A Gentle P

through the

Twelve Principles

Living the Values Behind the Steps

Patrick Carnes, Ph.D.

Hazelden Publishing

Hazelden Publishing
Center City, Minnesota 55012
hazelden.org/bookstore

ISBN: 978-1-59285-841-5

Library of Congress Cataloging-in-Publication Data
is on file at the Library of Congress.

Editor's note

The names, details, and circumstances may have been changed to protect the privacy of those mentioned in this publication.

This publication is not intended as a substitute for the advice of health care professionals.

Alcoholics Anonymous, AA, and the Big Book are registered trademarks of Alcoholics Anonymous World Services, Inc.

16 17 18 19 20   6 7 8 9 10

Cover design by David Spohn
Interior design and typesetting by Kinne Design

to Suzanne Louise Carnes
1945–2010

"Hi, I am Pat recovering with Suzanne."

It is customary in Recovering Couples Anonymous to introduce your-self within the context of your relationship. Thus for years I introduced myself with Suzanne as my partner. Much of what I have learned was with the leaven and seasoning of our life together. It seems fitting to dedicate this book to her to honor the myriads of ways she added to my own recovery journey.

Suzie and I had seven children. I had four and she had three, and all have now become a great family community. There are ten grand-children, who do keep things in a swirl. But they all are center to my world. I know they join me in acknowledging the extraordinary presence of Suzie as Grandmother, Mother, and Wife/Mate.

Contents

Acknowledgments vii

Introduction: From Steps and Rules to Principles and Recipes................ 1

Prologue: The Neuroscience Behind the Twelve Principles 9

Part I: Making Sense 17

   1. Principle One: Acceptance: What are my limits? 21

   2. Principle Two: Awareness: How do I know what is real? 43

   3. Principle Three: Spirituality: Am I loveable to God and others? 59

   4. Principle Four: Responsibility: Who am I? 77

   5. Principle Five: Openness: How do I trust? 101

Part II: Creating Congruence 119

   6. Principle Six: Honesty: What must improve? 121

   7. Principle Seven: Courage: What risks must I take? 147

   8. Principle Eight: Commitment: How am I responsible? 163

   9. Principle Nine: Responsiveness: What is integrity? 179

Part III: Growing Vision 193

   10. Principle Ten: Trust: How do I live not knowing outcomes? 195

   11. Principle Eleven: Meaning: What is the purpose of my life? 209

   12. Principle Twelve: Generativity: How do I pass it on? 227

Part IV: Living Into the Principles 245

   13. The Twelve Principles Day by Day 247

   14. Problem Solving with the Twelve Principles 253

Epilogue 263

Appendices 265

    A. Twelve Steps with Twelve Principles   265

    B. Twelve Step Support Group Information   267

    C. Recovery Resources from Dr. Patrick Carnes and Associates   271

Bibliography 273

About the Author 277

Acknowledgments

I WANT TO ACKNOWLEDGE the efforts of Sid Farrar and the staff of Hazelden for working hard around the realities of losing a spouse. Similarly, I will always be grateful to Debbie Sanford of Pine Grove Behavioral Health and the staff of the Gentle Path Program for their unstinting support during that same process. No one had to make more adjustments than the staff of the International Institute for the Training of Addiction and Trauma (IITAP) and the Certified Sex Addiction Therapy Community (CSAT). I am particularly grateful for the grace and competence of my daughter Stefanie Carnes, who stepped into the breach in so many personal and professional ways. This book would not be what it is without the collective efforts of Scott Edelstein, Pennie Johnson, and Suzanne O'Connor. Scott brought coherence to the book, and Pennie and Suzanne vetted and deepened the substance that Scott was able to simplify and distill. Together they were a wonderful work group.

From Steps and Rules to Principles and Recipes

TWELVE STEPS. TWELVE TRADITIONS. Embedded in both is a set of Twelve Principles for maintaining our focus, deepening our recovery, measuring our progress, and living lives of sanity and serenity.

Most of us start a Twelve Step program as a way to stay sober or change a specific behavior. Over time, the Twelve Steps open us to support and awareness, and help us see that we're not able to make the necessary changes by ourselves. In order to swim upstream, we need to ask for help from other people and from our Higher Power. Only with this help, and through working our Twelve Step program every day, are we able to change our lives.

As we continue in recovery over the months and years, most of us also discover that we have more than one addiction, and that these addictions act together, triggering each other. As we work to establish sobriety, at times we feel like we're playing a game of Whack-a-Mole: once we successfully manage one addiction, another reasserts itself, demanding our attention. Day by day, however, through the power of the Twelve Steps, we re-engineer our life. We learn how to stay focused and how to keep our brain in balance. Working the Steps propels us into discovery and growth.

Over the past seventy-five years, a similar process of growth and discovery has taken place with the Twelve Steps themselves. At first the Steps were only for alcoholics in AA and for their loved ones participating in Al-Anon. By the 1950s, however, we also had Narcotics

Anonymous and Alateen for young people. ACoA, for the adult children of alcoholics, followed in the 1970s, as did CoDA for co-dependents (also called coaddicts) in the 1980s. Today there are dozens of Twelve Step groups for people whose lives have become unmanageable in relation to not only alcohol and other drug dependence but also addictive and compulsive behaviors such as eating, sex, relationships, work, exercise, gambling, and spending, as well as mental health disorders, co-occurring with addictions or in and of themselves.

Over these years, our understanding of the Twelve Steps—and the wisdom and science behind them—has evolved and deepened considerably, creating some dramatic changes in Twelve Step life. We now know, for example, that the great majority of addicts (some studies say over eighty percent) have two or more addictions. We also know that the Twelve Steps work in exactly the same way for every type of addiction, that multiple addictions need to be treated together, and that addiction and mental illness often (though not inevitably) go hand in hand. It has also become clear that as people have successfully learned to use the Steps to overcome different addictions and problems, people in the various Twelve Step fellowships have much to offer each other.

When my book *A Gentle Path through the Twelve Steps* was first published in 1993, these simple ideas were considered revolutionary by some and heretical by others. Since then, however, these ideas have become widely accepted by scientists, medical and mental health professionals, clergy, and the general public. Just as that book inspired (and became part of) the evolution of Twelve Step work, it also pointed to what might come after it. As the interconnections among Twelve Step fellowships have grown, so has the need to move beyond the rules, lists, and slogans that make up much of Twelve Step life, especially as people move past the early stages of recovery. Helpful as these are, we can limit our recovery if we apply their wisdom only in a rigid or dogmatic way. Rigidity deprives the Twelve Steps of some of their vital force, and deprives us of some of the Steps' most important life lessons.

I have also seen firsthand a great hunger among people in recovery for something that picks up where *A Gentle Path through the Twelve Steps* leaves off. During the 1990s and 2000s, I led a series of weekend retreats for people in leadership roles who had been in recovery for several years. We met once a quarter for twelve quarters. At the end of the three-year program, people said, "We don't want to leave. We want to go deeper." These folks knew they needed a curriculum to guide them on the next leg of their journey of recovery. It quickly became clear to me that they were not alone.

Over time, I also came to realize that Twelve Step communities have a problem. Although they offer us many wonderful things to study and read, some folks spend five, ten, or fifteen years in recovery before somebody says to them, "You know, you ought to read *this*" or "Have you taken a look at *this*?" It is wasteful, if not outright tragic, that people often encounter many useful tools and ideas only by accident, or trial and error.

Furthermore, for many people, simply going to meetings and finding a sponsor is not enough. Especially if the meeting becomes stagnant or is otherwise not a functional one—or if you and your sponsor are not well matched or remain stuck repeating the same ideas and practices—then the recovery process can be weakened or undermined. Worse, many people who go to meetings conscientiously for years never get the full benefits because they are never given a map. Indeed, for many recovering folks there *is* no map beyond Step work. They learn only what percolates down through their sponsor, their group, and perhaps a therapist.

I have long felt that many people who have been in recovery for a year or more need a book that condenses and presents the essentials of long-term recovery in a practical, deliberate way. Such a book ought to provide a curriculum to help create more robust recoveries, fewer and briefer relapses, and greater serenity. *A Gentle Path through the Twelve Principles* is that book.

The Twelve Principles serve as the natural lens for this curriculum, since they are embedded in every Step and every Tradition. The Steps naturally unfold into the Principles, which combine structure with flexibility, and depth with simplicity and clarity. The Twelve Principles help us to make a paradigm shift. We move from rules to recipes, letting go of our old ways of thinking and acting, and accepting that change in our life is both ongoing and inevitable. The Principles become our map to a new way of living, as well as the engine that makes this new life happen.

The Twelve Principles themselves are not new and are possibly the greatest assets of Twelve Step programs. Unlike the Steps and Traditions, they exist in multiple forms and variations—all quite similar, but not strictly defined. The ones used here are distilled from various versions used by different fellowships over the years. Anyone who lives a Twelve Step life will recognize them immediately. When practiced earnestly, these Principles help us to develop an essential skill set for life.

If we stay with recovery long enough, we absorb these Principles naturally as part of Twelve Step culture. Over time, we automatically apply them more and more to our lives. Making them explicit, however, helps speed up important connections and deepens the learnings that are at the heart of recovery. Careful study of the Twelve Principles helps us connect the dots. That connecting is the purpose of this book. Furthermore, embedded within each of the Twelve Principles are multiple strategies, tools, and insights. This book unpacks them.

Principles vs. Rules

Principles represent a higher level of learning and thinking than rules or guidelines do. A rule is something to follow, usually in the precise way prescribed, but a principle is something to reflect on, implement, and live into. Rules are typically remembered and recited verbatim; principles are *experienced* in our hearts, guts, and brains.

Like recipes, the Twelve Principles allow for some variation and modification. You can follow a recipe for pancakes to the letter, or you can add more blueberries (or more flour or more eggs) to create something slightly different but delicious and nourishing nonetheless. Still, there are limits: replace the blueberries with codfish and your pancakes become unmanageable. Furthermore, sometimes recipes *need* to be modified. If you're baking bread at 8,000 feet, you need to alter the recipe to get the same results you would at sea level.

We folks in recovery often have difficulty managing our feelings. We hate the discomfort of being upset or afraid or angry. We also typically try to avoid uncertainty, which can cause us great anxiety. Unfortunately, one way many of us deal with anxiety and uncertainty is by turning flexible principles into rigid rules. We make them sacred or even sacramental, thus creating needless trouble for ourselves and others. If you catch yourself doing this with the Twelve Principles, remind yourself that this is one more form of stinking thinking, and talk with your sponsor or someone else you trust in the program. Also remind yourself that the Principles offer us the most benefit, and the most hope, when we let them live inside us as healthy, adaptable organisms.

Unlike the Twelve Steps or the Serenity Prayer, the Twelve Principles are not a set of texts to be memorized or recited. Instead, they are a paradigm: a way of viewing and being in the world. Putting the Principles into practice in our lives shifts our internal paradigm; the rules, beliefs, and processes through which we perceive things go through a fundamental change.

What's to Come

Although this book is built around the Twelve Principles, it is not limited to them.

We'll begin with a look at the neuroscience behind the Principles. We now know, for example, that the basic neurology of recovery involves literally re-growing our brains, creating new and healthier ways of thinking, perceiving, and acting, eventually building new neural pathways to sustain those behaviors and thought patterns. Next we'll dig into the Twelve Principles, devoting a chapter to each, and look at how each one relates to the relevant Step. We'll also ask the essential question embedded in each Principle. Here are the Steps, each with its correlative Principle and key question.

The Twelve Steps of Alcoholics Anonymous

Step	Principle	Key Question
Step One We admitted we were powerless over alcohol—that our lives had become unmanageable.	Acceptance	What are my limits?
Step Two Came to believe that a Power greater than ourselves could restore us to sanity.	Awareness	How do I know what is real?
Step Three Made a decision to turn our will and our lives over to the care of God *as we understood Him.*	Spirituality	Am I loveable to the God of my understanding and others?
Step Four Made a searching and fearless moral inventory of ourselves.	Responsibility	Who am I?
Step Five Admitted to God, to ourselves, and to another human being the exact nature of our wrongs.	Openness	How do I trust?
Step Six Were entirely ready to have God remove all these defects of character.	Honesty	What must improve?
Step Seven Humbly asked Him to remove our shortcomings.	Courage	What risks must I take?

continued

Step	Principle	Key Question
Step Eight Made a list of all persons we had harmed, and became willing to make amends to them all.	Commitment	How am I responsible?
Step Nine Made direct amends to such people wherever possible, except when to do so would injure them or others.	Responsiveness	What is integrity?
Step Ten Continued to take personal inventory and when we were wrong promptly admitted it.	Trust	How do I live, not knowing outcomes?
Step Eleven Sought through prayer and meditation to improve our conscious contact with God *as we understood Him,* praying only for knowledge of His will for us and the power to carry that out.	Meaning	What is the purpose of my life?
Step Twelve Having had a spiritual awakening as a result of these steps, we tried to carry this message to alcoholics, and to practice these principles in all our affairs.	Generativity	How do I pass it on?

The Twelve Steps are reprinted and adapted with permission of Alcoholics Anonymous World Services, Inc. Permission to reprint and adapt this material does not mean that AA has reviewed or approved the content of this publication, nor that AA agrees with the views expressed herein. AA is a program of recovery from alcoholism only. Use of the Twelve Steps and Twelve Traditions in connection with programs and activities which are patterned after AA, but which address other problems, does not imply otherwise.

In chapter 13 we'll explore some simple ways to make the most of the Principles day by day; in chapter 14 we'll look at how the Twelve Principles can be used to solve everyday problems.

Giving Thanks

Our planet is rapidly moving to a system of pooled wisdom (think of Wikipedia or your favorite blog). The same is happening in the Twelve Step world, where fellowships are sharing their insights through their writings, websites, blogs, and all-fellowship meetings. This is a grand and wonderful network of communities that have been opened to us, because we all get better when we pool our experience.

This book, too, contains much pooled wisdom. I have drawn from many different Twelve Step fellowships and fellowship manuals and textbooks (such as AA's Big Book) as well as from multiple researchers, studies, and disciplines. As for the pithy and inspiring quotations throughout this book, these come from the entire panorama of human wisdom. The exercises can be done in this book using the lines and spaces provided, with additional pages added as needed, or if you prefer, you can buy a journal or notebook and recreate the exercises there.

Like *A Gentle Path through the Twelve Steps*, this book is continually in progress. There will surely be later editions, expansions, and commentaries on websites and blogs, and I welcome suggestions for potential improvements. To make suggestions, please visit patrickcarnes.com, where you'll also find an ever-evolving array of Twelve Step tools, exercises, and other helpful items. To deepen your practice of the principles, go to www.thetwelveprinciples.com and become a partner in the process. This website provides free additional materials and leadership instructions for use by Twelve Step communities. It is donation-supported, and all profits support the American Foundation for Addiction Research (AFAR) and other recovery support organizations.

— Patrick J. Carnes

The Neuroscience Behind the Twelve Principles

IN THE TWENTY-FIRST CENTURY, we know something that Bill W., Dr. Bob, and the other founders of AA intuited but couldn't prove scientifically. We know how and why recovery works.

What the founders of AA discovered through trial, error, luck, and grace has now been validated by science. Recent developments in neuroscience, radiology, genetics, and psychobiology give us a clear picture of how addiction hijacks the human brain. They also give us equally clear evidence that working a Twelve Step program literally rewires our brains for recovery. Through CT scans, MRIs, and other high-tech tools, we now know that:

- Addiction changes the brain, deadening certain cognitive areas and laying down neural networks that chemically encourage us to compulsively repeat harmful behaviors.

- All addictions, including those that do not involve alcohol or other drugs, create similar wounds in the same centers of the brain.

- Addictions interact in the brain in several different ways. One addiction can trigger, replace, or heighten another through a measurable biochemical process.

- Trauma—whether physical, sexual, or emotional—changes the brain's chemistry, predisposing it to addictions and compulsions.

- The new thoughts and behaviors produced by working the Twelve Steps appear to heal the brain in observable, predictable ways, building and deepening new neural pathways.

- As these neural pathways deepen, we create new, healthy patterns of thinking and acting.

- No matter how addicted we are or how unmanageable our life has become, our brains retain the potential for healing and recovery in their very cells.

- Safety is a prerequisite for healing the brain. Only when the brain "feels" safe—when it isn't functioning in a crisis mode—can it optimally reconstruct itself.

These breakthroughs paint a vivid picture of what happens in recovery. Combined, they verify the original insights of the AA founders in 1935. They also explain why people who leave Twelve Step programs and don't find similar guidelines for changing their thinking and behaviors usually fall back into addiction. Let's look at some of the many ways in which the brain's chemistry and biology affect our recovery.

The Hijacked Brain

Addiction hijacks our brain. Over time it damages the brain so that it consistently makes harmful choices, even when we don't want it to. Think back to the days before your recovery began. You would plan and intend to do one thing, sometimes with great resolve. Yet, despite your best efforts and intentions, you would nevertheless do something different, and harmful.

Brain scans have revealed the neurochemistry behind this. All addictions partially damage or disrupt the frontal lobes, the parts of the brain responsible for judgment, discernment, and common sense. This disruption is biological; it has nothing to do with a lack of will or poor moral judgment. These biological changes require significant biological healing. This healing takes time, and closely parallels the healing of a stroke victim's brain. As neuroscientist Bryan Kolb explains, people with addictions or strokes can't just sit back and wait for the brain to heal itself. Deliberate, ongoing effort is essential. As Dr. Kolb puts it, "Grab the frontal lobes and don't let go."

The Twelve Principles are vitally important in recovery because they help us focus ongoing energy and attention on healing. They also give us a recipe for sticking with recovery over the long term. In addition, they provide a framework for living a sane and serene life. This framework is built on universal psychological and spiritual principles that work for everyone, not just people in recovery.

The Twelve Principles and the Brain

Working the Twelve Steps can take us to a place of safety, sanity, and serenity. But the Twelve Steps are the beginning of a journey, not a destination. Over time, as our recovery deepens, we need to internalize and practice the Principles that are suggested by the Steps ever more in our affairs.

Principles require a higher level of thinking and learning than any rule, because a principle requires both reflection and mindful implementation. As a result, principles use far more of the bandwidth of our brains, and more oxygen and energy as well. It takes almost no thought or energy to follow a sign's instructions to "Keep off the grass," but it takes discernment, humility, focus, and self-awareness to practice courage.

The Twelve Principles also help us integrate the many different areas of the brain. This is an observable biological process, not a metaphor. Full integration requires thousands of hours of focused effort —typically five years or more of working the Steps and practicing the Principles. And this is really only laying the foundation for what is a life-long process and journey.

To the brain, recovery is very similar to learning a new language. At first we focus on learning the basics: vocabulary, pronunciation, and the placement of nouns and verbs in learning a language correspond to becoming aware of all the ways our thinking gets hijacked, how our addiction harms other people, and so on. Over time, however, as our fluency builds, we begin to naturally do the next right thing—picking the correct word or putting our sentences in the proper order corresponds to being honest with ourselves and others, recognizing and acknowledging our feelings, empathizing with and accepting other people, and so on. Eventually the new language—or, for those of us in recovery, the thoughts and behaviors engendered by the Twelve Principles—become fully integrated into our neural wiring.

This wiring is not just in one part of our brain. Until recently, scientists thought that the part of the brain known as the *hippocampus* was the seat of all our emotions. Brain scans have revealed, however, that we all have very long chains of brain cells that appear to weave back and forth around the hemispheres of our brain, starting on one side of our head and ending up on the other. These carry information and the capacity to experience emotion all over the brain. It turns out that our emotions aren't localized in any one part of the brain; they're built into our brain's organizational structure. Our emotions also may partly reside in other parts of our body. It now appears that every human heart has cells that are involved with our experience of certain emotions. We often say that we know something in our hearts: It turns out that this may be literally true.

Addictive Emotions

Perhaps the most startling recent discovery about the brain is that *feelings themselves can be addictive.* This is true not only of pleasurable emotions, but of anger, fear, despair, loneliness, grief, and other painful emotions as well. When you give in to road rage, you energize your own brain with neurochemicals that are part of the brain's stress response. Those chemicals juice up the brain's reward centers, which is why it feels so "good" to get angry. *The feelings and cravings created by these neurochemicals themselves are highly addictive.*

This also explains why people often cultivate and cling to painful emotions. They are unwilling to give up feeling bad because these unpleasant emotions create a shortcut to the brain's reward centers. We end up addicted to our own unhappiness, and this addiction can then interact with other addictions or compulsions.

There are several proven methods and practices for intervening with and rewiring these destructive emotional pathways:

- Creating stillness through meditation, journaling, etc.
- Telling your story
- Practicing positive self-talk
- Reconnecting with others

Creating Stillness

Hundreds of studies have demonstrated that we can heal our brain, temper our emotions, reduce our stress, and increase our serenity by practicing stillness: being quiet, alone, and present to ourselves. Mindfulness meditation, whereby we sit quietly watching our breath and thoughts without judgment, is one of the more effective ways that people have achieved this.

Stillness can involve other forms of meditating, praying, writing in a journal, or just relaxing quietly in nature. (Reading, browsing the Internet, and watching videos all focus our attention externally, so they don't qualify.) Our brain needs thirty to ninety minutes of stillness each day in order to heal optimally and operate at its best.

Telling Your Story

Each of us has an internal narrative about our life. We use this narrative as a way to see the world and explain it to ourselves. In recovery, we regularly rewrite and retell our story so that it includes new perceptions, understandings, and conclusions. Recent science has revealed that as we do this, we appear to actually rewire our brain by building new, more functional neural pathways. Over time, as we continue to rewrite and retell our story to ourselves and others, it makes sense that we would strengthen and deepen those pathways, providing ever more support for our recovery.

Telling our story to others also helps our brains in another way. Our brains contain nerve cells called *mirror neurons* that appear to be the biological corollary to our ability to put ourselves in others' shoes and respond emotionally to their experiences. Brain scans have revealed the mirror neurons in two people's brains seem to take on the same patterns when they report feeling emotionally connected to each other. In feeling connected to others, we also help heal our brain.

Practicing Positive Self-Talk

There's another form of self-talk besides telling our stories that can help us in our recovery: mindful inner dialog. This involves having mindful conversations in our head with different parts of ourselves, with our emotions, with people who are unavailable to us in person, and with particular problems or situations. These conversations can be purely mental, but we can also speak them aloud or write them out. In this book you'll be encouraged to have several of these conversations with your inner addict, with your feelings, and with some difficulties you hope to solve.

Mindful inner dialog is deeply important to changing and healing the brain. It helps the brain to relax and become open to new solutions and ideas. When I get stuck, I sometimes convene a mental panel of the different therapists I've had. I imagine them sitting around a table with me, and I ask them questions and listen carefully to their answers. This imaginary conversation often reveals a solution or observation that I'd overlooked, and wouldn't have been able to access in any other way.

I've often suggested this process of internal dialog to patients, and the feedback I have received affirms the value of this process. My patients discovered that they have more insight about themselves than they realized. They learn to access parts of their brains that had previously been out of reach.

Reconnecting with Others

As we practice the Twelve Principles, we gain more experience in telling the truth and having difficult conversations with others. Some of these involve making sincere apologies and amends. Some require us to challenge prevailing beliefs, other people, or ourselves. Some demand that we set or reset personal boundaries. Some involve ending or redefining old relationships. Virtually all such conversations strengthen our brain's mirror neuron systems, build empathy, and help us to work out whatever we're struggling with.

Your Inner Observer

The healing practices described on the previous pages—practicing mindful stillness, telling your story, talking to yourself, and having difficult conversations with others—all help to create an *inner observer*. This is an internal chief operating officer that mindfully observes the functioning of all other parts of the brain.

Our inner observer can warn us when our addiction is trying to seduce us; when we have fallen into stinking thinking; when we are afraid, anxious, or stressed; when we have the urge to flee or hide; or when we need to ask for help. Our inner observer can also remind us to tell the truth, to stay present in the midst of painful and difficult emotions, to recall the wisdom of the Twelve Steps and Twelve Principles, and to do the next right thing. Our inner observer is our seat of self-awareness. Over time, as we practice the Twelve Principles in all our affairs, it can also become a source of wisdom and a vital force for self-transcendence.

Freeing Up Your Brain's Bandwidth

One of the simplest but most powerful results of living by the Twelve Principles is freedom. Addicts' lives are full of inconsistencies. We say one thing but do another. We live secret lives. We lie. We do things that are inconsistent with how we present ourselves to the world. We have so many things to keep track of—multiple lies, stories, promises, and lives.

The Twelve Principles are all about consistency. When we practice these Principles in all our affairs, what we believe, what we say, and what we do all match up. As a result, we no longer have to keep track of anything but reality. This frees up a great deal of our emotional and intellectual bandwidth for engaging fully with life, and for doing the next right thing. By now it should be clear that everything in this book aligns closely with recent discoveries in brain science. It all aligns just as closely with recent advances in psychotherapy. Neither science nor therapy is our enemy; when practiced properly, each can provide recipes for creating discernment and wisdom.

As you make your way through the readings and exercises that follow, please remember that this book, too, is a recipe. Feel free to adapt it in ways that you feel will be helpful. Also keep in mind that a recipe does more than just create something tasty and nutritious; it also helps you learn to be a better cook. Lastly, throughout this book be gentle with yourself. No one else can do that for you.

❦

Part I

❦

Making Sense

Recovery is, among many positive things, a process of making sense of our life. When we were in the throes of our addiction, much of what we did made no sense to others. Sometimes it made no sense even to our addiction-damaged brain. By the time we were ready for recovery, our whole life no longer made sense.

In recovery, as we work the Steps and live according to the Principles, we begin to see the world in an entirely new light. Things start to make sense again. Meanwhile, as we renew our brain cells, we also create new, healthier organs of sensibility. We cease denying reality and start to see things as they always have been. We embrace new ideas and viewpoints. Sometimes we get an essential insight that leads to three or four others. In turn, these open us up to something still bigger, creating what psychologists call a *transformational cascade.* A key task in recovery is to keep that cascade going.

This whole process closely parallels both therapy and spiritual growth, and it continues for as long as we maintain our recovery. There is no endpoint to learning and growth.

This process guides us through three distinct stages. Although all of us can practice the Twelve Principles at any time, certain Principles naturally predominate in each stage. Let's look at these three stages and the ways in which the Twelve Principles are woven into them.

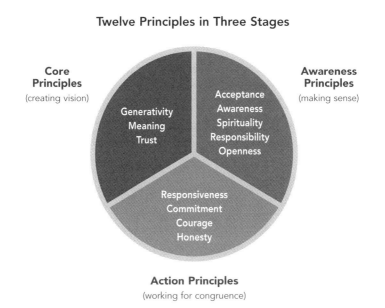

Twelve Principles in Three Stages

Core Principles
(creating vision)

Generativity
Meaning
Trust

Acceptance
Awareness
Spirituality
Responsibility
Openness

Awareness Principles
(making sense)

Responsiveness
Commitment
Courage
Honesty

Action Principles
(working for congruence)

In our early recovery, we move through this circle like the hands of a clock, beginning at the top, where the number twelve would be. Each Principle, and each stage, builds upon and includes the ones that come before it. Working the Twelve Steps for the first time takes us through all of the Principles, emphasizing them in the order presented in the circle. As we maintain our recovery, we will continue to regularly revisit all the Principles, though no longer in any particular sequence.

The first stage of living into the Twelve Principles involves making sense of the world and our life. This stage embodies Principles One through Five: acceptance, awareness, spirituality, responsibility, and openness. In this first stage, we let go of our fantasies about who we are, how the world works, and what (and who) we can control. Humbly and openly, we seek to replace those fantasies with reality, even when reality turns out to be difficult and painful.

This search for reality prompts us to seek answers to these questions:

- What are my limits?
- How do I know what is real?
- Am I loveable to God and others?
- Who am I?
- How do I trust?

We of course do not find these answers by trying to get them from some wise sage, oracle, or sponsor. We discover them one day at a time by living our lives and applying the Twelve Principles as best we can.

• • •

CHAPTER ONE

Principle One: Acceptance

{ What are my limits? }

| Step One. | *We admitted we were powerless over our addiction—that our lives had become unmanageable.* |

ACCEPTANCE IS THE most fundamental of the Twelve Principles. It is the foundation on which the other eleven Principles are built. Acceptance is about acknowledging our limits. What we can and cannot do. What we can and cannot control. What we can and cannot know. Where we have power and where we don't. What things other people can do that we can never do again—drink alcohol, for example, or play the slots. Acceptance means saying yes to life in its entirety. It is saying no to the delusions that have made life unmanageable. It is a commitment to reality at all costs.

Acceptance often means letting go of what we want or expect. This almost always hurts. But it hurts less than living in fantasy or denial, because reality always trumps illusory beliefs, hopes, and desires.

Acceptance often involves grief because it requires us to give something up: a dream, a goal, a cherished idea, a story or explanation about how things are, or a way of thinking or living or being. We

Acceptance is not submission; it is acknowledgement of the facts of a situation. Then deciding what you're going to do about it.

— KATHLEEN CASEY THEISEN

often achieve acceptance only after working our way through four stages of grief: denial, anger, bargaining, and depression. The good news is that when we reach the stage of depression, acceptance often follows close behind, and with acceptance comes serenity.

It is no coincidence that acceptance is the very bedrock of the Serenity Prayer: "God, grant me the serenity to accept the things I cannot change, courage to change the things I can, and wisdom to know the difference." In the first phrase, we accept our limitations. In the second, we accept our power and our responsibility to act. In the third, we accept our need to discern.

Acceptance requires both willingness and courage. It often requires us to stay in the midst of difficulty, pain, or confusion, rather than obeying our urge to flee. Yet acceptance also requires us to be gentle, especially with ourselves. We practice acceptance when we say any of the following: "I don't know." "I'm sorry." "I was wrong." "I don't understand." "Please help me." "Please teach me." "I can't do this alone."

The Key Question of Acceptance: What Are My Limits?

For us addicts, acceptance begins when we admit our powerlessness over our addiction and the unmanageability of our life. But as we continue in recovery, we learn that acceptance involves so much more.

Over time, we learn to accept that we are flawed and limited, simply because we are human. We learn to accept that there are many things we cannot do and innumerable things we cannot know. We learn to be clear and honest about our limitations, discovering what they are and living within them. We learn how to ask for what we need, how much is enough, and how much is too much.

It's possible to have sex with many different people, but we know that someone will probably get hurt if we do. We can work many extra hours to build a business or earn a promotion, but we know that if we neglect our family or our health, we create harm. We realize that if we spend more money than we make, we invite chaos into our financial life. We see that if we become enmeshed with another person, that person's problems become ours. And we understand that if our lifestyle demands more from us than we can give, we set ourselves up for relapse.

We addicts can easily lose ourselves in sex, or work, or money, or intimacy with another person, or a particular lifestyle. We need to learn and accept our limits in each area, and then manage and monitor ourselves carefully to stay within those limits. When we can't, we need to ask for assistance.

In recovery we learn that many things in life are impossible for us to do alone, yet they often become possible when we ask for and accept help. When we do need help, we learn to ask for it from other people, from our Higher Power, or both. We also learn to stand on our own two feet when we can. And over time, we develop the wisdom to know when to do each one. As our recovery continues, we also learn to accept our most basic limitation: our own death. Some day—perhaps tomorrow, perhaps today; we can't know when—we will pass out of this world.

------------------------- ❁ -------------------------

Some people confuse acceptance with apathy, but there's all the difference in the world. Apathy fails to distinguish what can and cannot be helped; acceptance makes that distinction. Apathy paralyzes the will-to-action; acceptance frees it by relieving it of impossible burdens.

— ARTHUR GORDON

You have to accept whatever comes and the only important thing is that you meet it with courage and with the best that you have to give.

— ELEANOR ROOSEVELT

Addiction Interaction

In Twelve Step life, the most fundamental form of acceptance is accepting the fact of our addiction or our multiple addictions. Most addicts have more than one addiction. Some have several. However, we may spend months or years in recovery before we accept—or become aware of—all of them. Most addictions don't involve alcohol or other drugs; instead, they involve processes (compulsive behaviors), emotions, or attachments. Addictions can also migrate, or "pass the baton." We can stop practicing one addiction and learn to manage its cravings, only to suddenly hear the call of a different addiction to replace that one—perhaps one we hadn't dealt with before.

The chart on the next page lists the four general families of addiction (substances, processes, feelings, and compulsive attachments) and the twenty-seven different addiction types.

After you have reviewed the four lists in this chart carefully, write your answers to the following questions.

Which of these addictions did you actively practice in the past?

Addiction Types

Substances

Alcohol

Cocaine

Methamphetamine

Nicotine

Heroin

Prescription drugs

Marijuana

Hallucinogens

Processes

Sex (including cybersex)

Work

Exercise

Video gaming

Eating (anorexia, bulimia, bingeing)

Spending money (gambling, shopping, e-trading)

Internet use

Feelings

Fear

Self-loathing

Excitement

Love/romance

Misery or despair

Compulsive Attachments

Pathological giving, rescuing, or becoming a hero

Creating drama, crises, and excitement

Managing the impression we have on others

Demonstrating codependency/coaddiction

Traumatic bonding (staying with dangerous or hurtful people)

Which ones do you practice now?

_____

_____

_____

_____

Which ones pull at you internally now? Of these, which ones could become a problem if you are not attentive to your recovery?

_____

_____

_____

_____

The Triggering Cascade

One addiction often triggers another. Stephan gets drunk, then heads downtown and hires a prostitute. After bingeing on candy bars, Rowena sticks her finger down her throat, vomits, and hurries to the gym to exercise for the next three hours.

But often the ways in which addictions interact can be much more subtle. Triggers can line up in a sequence, with one trigger leading to another. Once the first trigger occurs, a whole cascade of actions can get activated. It can be very difficult to break free of this cascade.

When Kim walks home from her subway stop and passes the office building where her ex-husband used to work, she is reminded of the times he forced her to have sex with him. A great wave of anger rises up inside her, and often she finds herself trembling and breathless. There is a casino halfway between the office building and her home, and sometimes Kim goes in to relax. The blinking, ringing slot machines help her calm down and take her mind off of her troubles, and the two-dollar drinks are a great bargain. Plus, it's always a minor thrill when she wins a jackpot. When she first began going to the casino, she went about once a week. Now she goes in almost every day after work, often staying until nearly midnight. She typically has three or four drinks and loses sixty to a hundred dollars a night.

It's not hard to see that Kim has a gambling addiction, and very likely a drinking problem as well. It's much less obvious that the addiction cascade begins with her memories of abuse, which are triggered by a particular location. One simple way Kim can circumvent this cascade is by using a different subway stop. It's an extra two-minute subway ride and an extra five-minute walk, but if she takes this alternate route, it discourages the cascade from starting.

How do addictive impulses interact in your own life? Think of the times, places, thoughts, images, or situations in which addiction beckons to you. Write these down.

_____

_____

_____

_____

_____

Next, ask yourself what often leads up to those times, places, thoughts, images, or situations. Write these down.

_____

_____

_____

_____

_____

Then ask yourself what you usually do—or are tempted to do—in response to each trigger. Write these down.

_____

_____

_____

_____

_____

Next, put all three of these lists together.

When I experience or encounter . . .	. . . I am tempted to respond by . . .	. . . which encourages me to . . .

Now look over these three lists. Do they describe the whole addictive cascade as you experience it? Are there additional steps in your cascade? If so, in the space below draw a map of the entire cascade.

I have accepted fear as a part of life—specifically the fear of change, the fear of the unknown; and I have gone ahead despite the pounding in my heart that says: turn back, turn back, you'll die if you venture too far.

— ERICA JONG

---- ❦ ----

You must accept the truth from whatever source it comes.

— MOSES MAIMONIDES

Accepting and Forgiving Yourself

When we do our initial First Step, we accept our powerlessness and the unmanageability of our life. But it isn't until Step Four that we begin to look fully and honestly at ourselves. Thereafter, we may accept who we are and what we have done, but may hate ourselves for it. We may also feel that we don't deserve our own forgiveness. We may struggle with shame and blame, saying to ourselves, *I've been such an awful person* or *How could I have done such a thing?* or *What I did was completely unforgivable.*

Now you are ready to deepen your acceptance into forgiveness. In the space on the next page, write a letter to yourself. This letter will be a covenant with yourself to not let shame or self-blame hinder your recovery. Please do the following:

- Reaffirm your acceptance of responsibility for the harm you caused when you practiced your addiction.

- Remind yourself that shame and self-blame get in the way of recovery, and that forgiveness strengthens it.

- Remind yourself that forgiveness—including self-forgiveness—is an act of courage.

- Write one to three sentences in which you fully forgive yourself.

When you are done, sign the letter. Then, to remind yourself of the covenant you have just made, photocopy the letter and post it somewhere where you will see it every day. In this letter you accept and forgive yourself as a fallible human being. You also practice gentleness and mercy with yourself.

Dear (your name),

_____

_____

_____

_____

_____

_____

_____

_____

_____

_____

_____

_____

_____

_____

_____

_____

_____

_____

_____

_____

———— ✿ ————

Everything we shut our eyes to, everything we run away from, everything we deny, denigrate or despise, serves to defeat us in the end. What seems nasty, painful, evil, can become a source of beauty, joy, and strength, if faced with an open mind. Every moment is a golden one for him who has the vision to recognize it as such.

— HENRY MILLER

Your Harshest Inner Voices

Just because you have made a covenant with yourself not to fall into shame or self-blame, the inner voices that routinely criticize and attack you won't suddenly go away. They may even get temporarily louder because you've promised that you won't take them very seriously.

As part of your recovery, it's important to accept the existence of these inner voices without accepting the validity of what they say. Please answer the questions below.

In what situations do your inner critics typically say harsh things about you?

_____

_____

_____

What do they say?

_____

_____

_____

How long do they usually keep this up?

_____

_____

_____

What are their underlying messages about who you are and what you have done?

_____

_____

_____

Where have you heard those same messages before? Who told you those things when you were younger?

_____

_____

_____

How accurate are those messages? What about them is untrue? What, if anything, about them is true?

_____

_____

_____

_____

_____

_____

It often helps to name these critical voices. For example, if one such voice repeats what your grandfather told you when you were young, name it Granddad. If another voice reminds you of your overly punitive math teacher, call it General Geometry. If a voice regularly demands, "Why can't you be more like your sister?" then call it Sister Disster.

Naming your inner critics helps you quickly recognize each one when it begins speaking to you. It also makes it easier to reply to each critic with an alternative message that's honest, accurate, and merciful. For example:

"So, Aunt Sophie, it's you again. You're talking trash, like always. The truth is, I was never just trying to get attention. When I was young, I was trying to find a way to get through the day without getting beaten. Now I do my best to let people know my needs and values. I'm sorry you aren't able see this."

"Norman, that's a load of crap and we both know it. I'm not a weak-willed wimp, and I haven't made a bargain with the Devil. I'm a fallible human being trying to live an honorable life. Sometimes I make mistakes, but they're honest ones. Now back off."

"Welcome back, You-Ruined-People's-Lives. Here's the deal: I'm sorry for all the harm I caused. I'll continue to make what amends I can and to work the Twelve Steps and practice the Twelve Principles as best I can. That's all I can do. If that's not good enough for you, that's your problem, not mine."

By responding to our inner critics in this way, we learn to be kind, merciful, and gentle with ourselves. In addition, when we make a mistake or something goes wrong, we become more able to catch ourselves before we smear ourselves with shame or blame.

On the lines on the next page, make a list of your most common inner critics. Briefly describe each one, then give it an easy-to-remember name.

Description	Name
_____	_____
_____	
_____	
_____	
_____	_____
_____	
_____	
_____	
_____	_____
_____	
_____	
_____	
_____	_____
_____	
_____	
_____	

❦

Accepting does not necessarily mean "liking," "enjoying," or "condoning." I can accept what is—and be determined to evolve from there. It is not acceptance but denial that leaves me stuck.

— NATHANIEL BRANDEN

Conversing with Your Inner Addict

Even though you have achieved months or years of sobriety, your inner addict remains an aspect of your psyche. A big part of acceptance is getting to know and accept this inner addict. This aspect of yourself may have access to important insights about you. Asking your inner addict questions may help you discover some new and valuable information about yourself.

Find a quiet spot where you can be alone and unobserved for half an hour. Pick up a pen or pencil and get into a comfortable position. If you like, imagine your inner addict standing or sitting in front of you; you can even pull up an extra chair. If you discover that your inner addict has a name, feel free to use it. Read each question below aloud; then become quiet and listen. Write down your inner addict's answer and add any additional reflections you may have.

Questions for My Inner Addict about Acceptance

What do I not understand about you? Is there some lesson you are still trying to teach me?

What emotional wounding drives you?

_____

_____

_____

_____

_____

_____

_____

_____

_____

What feelings of mine make me most vulnerable to you?

_____

_____

_____

_____

_____

_____

_____

_____

_____

Living a Life of Acceptance

If I could define enlightenment briefly,
I would say it is "the quiet acceptance of what is."
— WAYNE DYER

At the end of each chapter on a Principle, you'll discover some simple, meaningful ways to use the principle to enhance your recovery.

I can practice more acceptance in my life by . . .

Sex

. . . letting myself be nurtured and cared for during sex.

. . . not trying to coerce my partner into having sex, or into doing something sexual that he or she doesn't want to do.

. . . not expecting or hurrying toward orgasm, but being fully present to what is happening right now.

Add other examples that apply to you.

_____

_____

_____

_____

_____

_____

Money

  . . . understanding that money is a finite resource, even for the wealthy.

  . . . accepting that there are limits to what problems money can solve and how much happiness it can bring me.

  . . . saying yes to an offer of financial help if I need it, but only if the offer is not an attempt to manipulate me.

Add other examples that apply to you.

_____

_____

_____

_____

Work

  . . . not trying to get my coworkers to approach their jobs in the same way I do.

  . . . following the rules of my workplace and job, even if I don't like them.

  . . . leaving my work at work and giving my full attention to my friends and family when I'm with them.

Add other examples that apply to you.

_____

_____

_____

_____

Intimacy

. . . asking others to tell me what they think and feel, rather than guessing or assuming the answer.

. . . honoring other people's feelings by not labeling them as wrong or unreasonable.

. . . saying no to a request I know I cannot fulfill or that would cause me resentment, even though I know the person will be disappointed.

Add other examples that apply to you.

_____

_____

_____

_____

Lifestyle

. . . getting regular exercise because I know that my health requires it.

. . . not cramming my schedule so full that I have no time for rest and reflection.

. . . finding pleasure in nature and conversation with others rather than expensive things and activities.

Add other examples that apply to you.

_____

_____

_____

_____

There are two rules on the spiritual path: begin and continue.

— SUFI SAYING

· · ·

*Many of life's treasures remain hidden from us
simply because we never search for them. Often we do not
ask the proper questions that might lead us to
the answer to all our challenges.*

— ANDY ANDREWS

· · ·

CHAPTER TWO

Principle Two: Awareness

{ How do I know what is real? }

Step Two. *Came to believe that a Power greater than ourselves could restore us to sanity.*

EACH OF US HAS THE capacity to pay attention to our senses, emotions, impulses, thoughts, and actions. We also have the capacity to clearly observe the world around us: its beauty, its danger, its design. This capacity goes by several names, including *attention* and *mindfulness*. I believe the most expansive, all-inclusive term, however, is *awareness*.

Addiction gives us tunnel vision and narrows our attention to those things that satisfy its demands, creating a poverty in our inner and outer lives. Recovery expands our attention—first beyond our addiction, then beyond our fear and stinking thinking, and ultimately far beyond ourselves, into deep awareness.

In Principle One, we accepted and surrendered to the irrevocable realities of our life—our addiction, our powerlessness, and the unmanageability of our life. We stopped living in fantasy and magical thinking. Now, with these no longer controlling us, we can begin to notice things as they are. It is no accident that acceptance leads to awareness. When we make an internal commitment to reality, we naturally want to become more aware. All of the Twelve Principles follow this logic: each expands on the ones that come before, and leads naturally to the ones that follow.

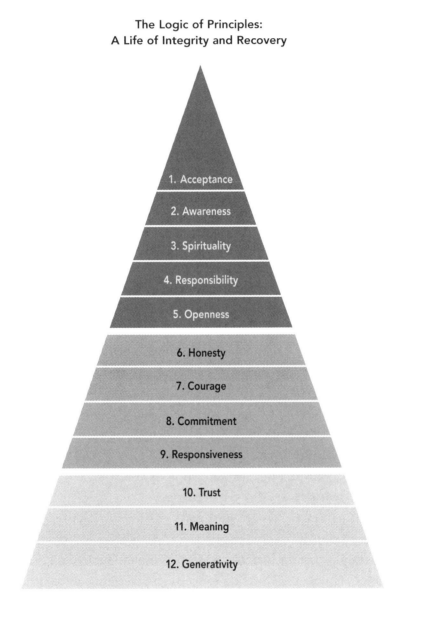

The Logic of Principles:
A Life of Integrity and Recovery

1. Acceptance
2. Awareness
3. Spirituality
4. Responsibility
5. Openness
6. Honesty
7. Courage
8. Commitment
9. Responsiveness
10. Trust
11. Meaning
12. Generativity

Andy Andrews has written a book about awareness called *The Noticer*. Its central character is an elderly man named Jones. Whenever Jones encounters someone, he notices the reality that the person isn't accepting and helps the person become more aware of it. This enables the person to get unstuck from long-term problems. A couple on the verge of divorce sees that the problem isn't each other, but their communication styles. A vagabond realizes for the first time that he's neither a victim nor a self-made failure. A business owner sees that his short-term decisions have long-range effects.

We, too, can change our lives dramatically by attending carefully to what goes on inside and outside us. As our inner observer practices paying attention, our fantasies lose their power and our reactivity subsides.

The Key Question of Awareness:
How Do I Know What Is Real?

As our awareness grows, we also begin noticing some wonderful and unsettling things about life.

Life is not random or meaningless.

We observe that events often come together in a helpful or meaningful—but often unpredictable and unexpected—way. Carl Jung called this process *synchronicity*. Events appear to have a purpose, even when they involve disappointment, struggle, or even disaster. The right people show up in our lives just when we need them. We see a Power greater than ourselves at work. We realize that we are not alone.

People travel to wonder at the height of mountains,
at the huge waves of the sea, at the long courses of rivers,
at the vast compass of the ocean, at the circular motion of
the stars; and they pass by themselves without wondering.

—SAINT AUGUSTINE

None of us knows what is going to happen.

Even as we recognize patterns and synchronicity, we also notice that the next moment is always uncertain and unpredictable. We are always in free fall, not knowing what the next day or moment will bring. We also realize, perhaps for the first time, that *life has always been this way*. The Twelve Steps and Twelve Principles support us in accepting this ever-present uncertainty, but they do not protect us from it.

We feel a call.

We see that our life matters, that everyone's life matters, and that there is purpose behind it all—though not necessarily a purpose that can be summed up in words. We also feel a personal call, direction, or responsibility—one that demands concrete action from us. At the time, in early recovery, this may simply be a call to recover from our addiction. Later in recovery as we begin to apply the Principles behind the Steps, it involves something more, such as a renewed commitment to our family, our work, or our life mission. Often this call appears in an entirely unexpected context, in what we might call a MacGuffin moment. The term *MacGuffin* was coined by film director Alfred Hitchcock. It originally referred to an event or situation that generated the central narrative of a film.

In recovery, especially after we've established our sobriety and freedom from the obsession with addictions, many of us experience our own spiritual MacGuffin moments. Suddenly we know what we need to do. We intuitively feel the importance of this call and the ways in which it connects us to others. We begin to feel that our life has a larger arc.

*Each day is a different one, each day brings a miracle of its own.
It's just a matter of paying attention to this miracle.*

—PAULO COELHO

MacGuffin moments are rarely moments of delight. Usually when we feel a call, it is not something we would ever choose; often it's precisely what we've tried to avoid. Yet when we hear a call, we must say yes to it. It will not give us peace until we do.

Moses did not want to lead the Israelites; he wanted his brother Aaron to take on that job. In *Lord of the Rings*, Frodo reluctantly leaves the Shire with the mysterious ring, and soon wishes he were back home. But the wizard Gandalf tells him, "We cannot choose the time we live in. We can only choose what we do with the time we are given."

Whatever form our particular call takes, it usually requires us to struggle and face difficulties. We may have to give up a cherished possession, belief, or relationship. These are all signals that the classic heroic journey has begun. For most of us, this journey won't involve thousand-mile ocean voyages, the rescuing of kidnapped princesses, or a search for immortality. More likely, it will be a call to get (or stay) married, or take a new job, or move, or begin volunteering for an important cause. But that does not make the journey any less heroic or less challenging.

As we mature in recovery, we often experience uncertainty, meaning, and a call all at once. This creates a spiritual paradox: we see that our life is following a meaningful arc, but we don't know what this arc is. Still, day by day, our life slowly starts to make sense.

The universe is not malevolent.

Albert Einstein observed that "The most important decision we make is whether we believe we live in a friendly or hostile universe." For many of us in recovery, this presents another paradox. Many of us have suffered at the hands of hostile or abusive people. We must not deny our past or try to sugarcoat or ignore life's dark side. As we work the Steps and Principles, however, we come to see that life calls us to grow rather than to simply suffer. Even in our struggles—sometimes *especially* in our struggles—we find wisdom and meaning.

The Jewish mystical tradition of Kabbalah contains an unusual creation story. God is lonely, so He creates human beings in the hope that, over time, they will develop enough awareness to keep company with Him. But the only way for humans to become this aware is to struggle with difficult challenges.

Buddhism offers a less poetic but similar observation. The Buddhist word for challenges and struggles is *dukkha*, which literally means "a wheel out of kilter." Buddhism doesn't propose that we try to get rid of challenges and struggles. Instead, it urges us to get comfortable with facing them, because they will always be a part of our life.

Awareness leads to sanity.

As our awareness grows, the focus of our life gradually shifts. We pay less attention to our own fantasies and magical thinking, and more to what is real. We stay alert for people who could become our guides, allies, and mentors. We spend less time in self-pity and more in gratitude. We expend less effort in trying to get things for ourselves and more in serving others. We recognize that what we want to avoid may be precisely what we need to embrace. We learn to face our fears, and the truth. In the process, our inner observer becomes wiser and more stable. It creates new mental pathways that enable it to think its way down into our feelings, and that enables feelings to rise up into our brain.

We also learn to pay attention to what matters, and to be less distracted by what doesn't. As a result, we find ourselves able to get more done, and do it better. We become more creative. We are able to generate more new ideas, approaches, and options for dealing with our challenges.

------------ ❦ ------------

The moment one gives close attention to any thing,
even a blade of grass, it becomes a mysterious, awesome,
indescribably magnificent world in itself.

— HENRY MILLER

Let us not look back in anger, nor forward in fear,
but around in awareness.

— JAMES THURBER

Flexing Your Awareness Muscles

Think back to a moment in your life when you were the most peaceful and serene. That "moment" may have lasted five seconds, five minutes, or five hours. It may have occurred when you were a small child, a year or two ago, or earlier today. Whatever and whenever it was, close your eyes and mentally return to it now. Picture it in as much detail as you can, using all of your senses. Then write down the details of this moment.

If you're like most people, you didn't have trouble remembering that marvelous moment in detail. That's because *all of us have an inherent ability to be aware.* When we're feeling happy and serene, most of us are naturally aware. When we're under stress or in pain, however, we can easily lose our awareness. Fortunately, all of us can improve our awareness in much the same way that we can build our muscles and train our memory.

Cultivating Awareness Exercise

Go to a quiet, comfortable spot where you can be alone. Bring a watch or clock with you. Sit in a relaxed position with your back fairly straight, so you don't wobble or start to fall asleep. Breathe normally. Close your eyes. For the next two minutes, pay attention to the input from your *senses:* the tastes in your mouth, the sounds in your ears, the smells in your nose, and the tactile sensations on and in your body.

Then turn your attention to your *feelings.* For two minutes, simply watch as your emotions rise and fall, appear and disappear. Don't try to grab onto them; don't try to push them away. Just observe them.

Then, for two minutes, simply follow your *impulses* as they bubble up and fade away. Watch each one calmly, without acting.

For the final two minutes, simply observe the *thoughts* that arise and recede in your mind. These will often be intertwined with impulses, emotions, and/or physical sensations.

---------------- ❦ ----------------

If we are too busy, if we are carried away every day by our projects, our uncertainty, our craving, how can we have the time to stop and look deeply into the situation—our own situation, the situation of our beloved one, the situation of our family and of our community, and the situation of our nation and of the other nations?

— THICH NHAT HANH

Open your eyes.

If you can, make this brief awareness practice a regular part of your day. The best times are in the morning, before your workday begins, and at night, shortly before going to bed. Also use this practice when you find yourself in a situation of high stress, strong emotion, or powerful impulses. Instead of quickly and automatically reacting, practice this awareness technique for 15–30 seconds. Have your inner observer simply notice what's going on in your brain and body—your physical sensations, emotions, impulses, and thoughts. Then, only after you have settled yourself in awareness, begin considering how you will choose to respond.

Everyone thinks of changing the world, but no one thinks of changing himself.

— LEO TOLSTOY

Terrible and Wonderful Moments

Think of three of the worst moments in your life—times when you were completely miserable or desperate. Maybe you felt that you were completely worthless, or were about to lose your mind, or might as well jump off a bridge. Describe these three moments briefly below.

1. _____

_____

_____

2. _____

_____

_____

3. _____

   _____

   _____

Now take a closer look at each of these moments, and see if it was in fact as awful as it felt. For each moment, please answer these questions: Did it force you to take action or make a decision? What was that action or decision? Did it change your life for the better? In what specific ways? Did it change anyone else's life for the better? In what ways?

_____

_____

_____

_____

_____

_____

Did it result in your encountering an important friend, ally, or guide? Who was this person? How and where did the encounter occur? What happened as a result of that encounter?

_____

_____

_____

_____

_____

_____

Did that moment point you toward recovery? Did it eventually lead to greater sanity and serenity? Briefly trace the sequence of events from that moment to your life today.

_____

_____

_____

_____

_____

_____

In that moment, were there clues that you were going to change your life and begin a heroic journey? If so, what were they? If you felt or heard a call, what form did it take?

_____

_____

_____

_____

_____

_____

------------------------- ✿ -------------------------

If we could see the miracle of a single flower clearly,
our whole life would change.

— BUDDHA

Conversing with Your Inner Addict

Find a quiet spot where you can be alone and unobserved for half an hour. Bring this book and a pen or pencil with you. Get comfortable, relaxed, and quiet. Reach out to your inner addict once again, perhaps imagining it in front of you or deep within your brain. Read the questions below aloud; then listen for your inner addict's answer to each one. Write down each answer and add any further reflections you may have.

Questions for My Inner Addict about Awareness

What are the most effective ways you distract me from my resolves? How do you try to coax me back into my old addictive cycle?

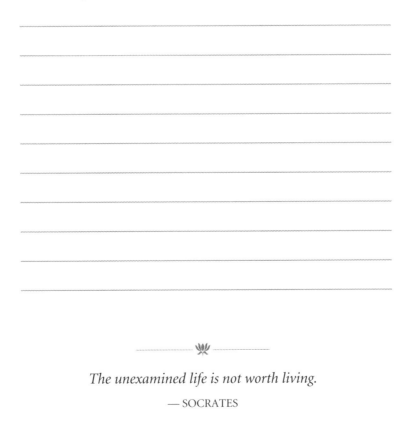

The unexamined life is not worth living.

— SOCRATES

How did you come to be? Why did you start? Who helped you?

_____

_____

_____

_____

_____

_____

_____

_____

_____

What have I not wanted to face about you being in my life?

_____

_____

_____

_____

_____

_____

_____

_____

_____

Living a Life of Awareness

Your vision will become clear only when you look into your heart.
Who looks outside, dreams. Who looks inside, awakens.

— CARL JUNG

I can practice more awareness in my life by . . .

Sex

. . . focusing on pleasurable feelings wherever they may appear, not just in my genitals.

. . . discovering what gives my partner pleasure, rather than doing what I think will give me pleasure.

. . . looking into my partner's eyes when we make love instead of keeping my eyes closed.

Add other examples that apply to you.

_____

_____

_____

_____

_____

Money

. . . keeping track of my finances so I'm aware of how much money I have, how much will come in (and when), and how much I can afford to spend.

. . . noticing when I have a sudden impulse to buy something, and then mentally stepping back and carefully considering the purchase before making a decision.

. . . being grateful for everything of value in my life, including my money, possessions, relationships, abilities, health, and sanity.

Add other examples that apply to you.

_____

_____

_____

_____

_____

Work

. . . noticing those tasks I want to put off or avoid and, instead, doing them and getting them out of the way.

. . . discovering what gives me satisfaction at work, and doing what I reasonably can to increase that satisfaction.

. . . watching my negative moods and reactions at work, and then discerning which ones are legitimate responses and which ones spring from my fears and fantasies.

Add other examples that apply to you.

_____

_____

_____

_____

_____

Intimacy

. . . paying close attention to what someone is saying without arguing, interrupting, or correcting.

. . . noticing when my partner (or friend or close relative) seems uneasy; asking gently, "What's going on for you right now? Is something bothering you?"; and then listening openly and nonjudgmentally to his or her answer.

. . . watching my own mind and stopping myself when I want to say something hurtful.

Add other examples that apply to you.

_____

_____

_____

_____

Lifestyle

. . . discovering what creates serenity for me, and what creates fear or anxiety.

. . . noticing the times of day when my energy and concentration are strongest, and when they are most fragile; scheduling tasks to best take advantage of this rhythm.

. . . spending regular time each day in meditation or reflection.

Add other examples that apply to you.

_____

_____

_____

_____

CHAPTER THREE

Principle Three: Spirituality

{ *Am I loveable to God and others?* }

ASK TWENTY PEOPLE what spirituality is and you'll get twenty different answers. Yet most definitions of spirituality include (or imply) four elements:

- Sharing pain
- Serving others
- Joining hands or forces
- Making a leap

Each of these is an act of love.

Sharing Pain

Our pain connects us to others' pain. As the Dalai Lama observed, if we had no pain, we would have no compassion.

When we suffer, we always suffer in our body. This is true even when our suffering is spiritual or emotional, because the neurons

Follow your bliss and the universe will open doors
for you where there are only walls.

— JOSEPH CAMPBELL

---

that create physical pain fire in both our brain and the rest of the body. Heartache is not a metaphor; nerve cells in our heart literally make us hurt. Suffering is always *felt*.

Our suffering also opens our heart to others' pain. Our brain is literally wired for empathy, for sharing pain, for connecting each hurt to other, similar hurts. Fear, grief, dread, despair—when we touch one deeply, often we touch them all. There's evidence that when we open ourselves to others' suffering, we grow special brain cells called *mirror neurons,* which, some scientists believe, enable us to literally feel—or at least empathize with—another person's pain.

Our suffering also opens our hearts to *ourselves.* Our life—everyone's life—is a tapestry woven partly from loss and pain. This is especially true in times of enormous change. During such times, when new pain touches old, it can flood our brain with emotions, especially if we've walled off the old pain for a long time. Suddenly all the unprocessed emotion comes flowing out. In these highly charged moments, we can turn to our inner observer. We can watch the pain as it arises without acting or reacting. We can feel it, accept it, be with it. We can have empathy and mercy for ourselves. We can observe the pain as it peaks, breaks, and begins to dissipate. Healing begins.

Serving Others

People who make a dramatic change in their work, spiritual, or community roles often talk of receiving a "call" as if having the decision come from a higher source. Few people (except perhaps workaholics) receive a call to relax on the couch and watch movies for a month.

A call requires us to risk ourselves, to do something different and unfamiliar. That often involves serving others—our family, our employer, a friend, our Twelve Step group, our community, our country.

In Sex Addicts Anonymous groups, whenever someone relapses, that person is immediately made the group's trusted servant. This is because *relapse always results from a focus on self rather than service.* Being appointed as a trusted servant becomes an immediate call to service and action. As our recovery grows, we discover that service is not a series of individual activities or roles. It is an ongoing commitment we make, day by day, and an expression of our love for others and ourselves.

Joining Hands or Forces

A call is almost always preceded (or accompanied) by a sense of things coming together. In some important way, the needs of the world line up with our internal compass and with our ability to make a positive difference. Suddenly we realize that things have changed. Or that things *need* to change. Or that *we* need to change. We also sense that, as part of our recovery, we *must* answer the call. And only we can answer it. No one else can answer it for us.

Yet other people can support us, guide us, teach us, and love us. When you answer your own call, you will have allies. Some will be folks who share your values, goals, and mission; some will simply care about you and want to support you. Reach out to these people and ask for their help.

You may also have some less obvious allies—people who ultimately help you in unexpected ways. A stubborn, abrasive coworker stands up for you and refuses to back down. Your judgmental aunt decides you've finally wised up and introduces you to influential people. Your abusive father-in-law, who has declared for years that you're dumb and lazy, suddenly loses his job and is devastated. This gives you the opportunity to step up and show that he can depend on you for help when he's down.

A Personal Example

My father started drinking again after thirty years of sobriety. Seeing him drink precipitated deep reactions in me, going back to the traumas of living with someone who started his day with an "eye opener." Obviously it precipitated family dynamics as well personal ones. But the personal ones were interfering with my own functioning. I went back into therapy, and my therapists felt it important for me to go into an inpatient setting so I could unravel and address the early traumas, which of course were the scaffolding of my addictions and relationship issues.

At the time, I had a Ph.D. in counseling and several books to my credit. I also had spent many hours in a therapist's office off and on as part of my recovery. When I walked into group, my case manager was waiting. Dressed in old jeans and cowboy boots, he did not look promising as a professional. Then on break I learned he had never completed high school. My arrogance kicked in. How was this going to work when I really needed help but probably knew more than the therapist? By the afternoon he intervened in my life in transformative ways. Today I look back on him as perhaps one of the best therapists in my experience. He in fact was my great ally in understanding my childhood.

The whole episode reminds me of that classic scene in the movie *Star Wars* when Luke Skywalker meets Yoda. He totally discounts Yoda as anyone who could help learn Jedi ways. When we are in free fall we often at first misperceive who our allies really are. It is one of the constants of all the great stories and of life that real help is not always obvious in free fall.

If you can see your path laid out in front of you step by step, you know it's not your path. Your own path you make with every step you take. That's why it's your path.

— JOSEPH CAMPBELL

Identifying Your Potential Allies

As you join forces with other people—your external allies—an *internal* joining of forces also takes place. Your inner observer surveys your inner and outer landscapes—your call, the needs of the world, your mission, your external allies, your courage, your internal self-talk—and puts all the pieces together. That observer's experience and insight also prompt it to reject things that might sabotage you—bad advice, toxic people, messages from your inner addict, magical thinking, impossible fantasies, and the like.

Once you have heard your own call, make a list of all the people you see as potential allies. Make several copies of the following list, My Potential Ally, and fill it out for each potential ally on your list.

My Potential Ally

Name: _____

Relationship to me: _____

How this person can help me as I answer my call:

_____

_____

_____

_____

What I will ask for:

_____

_____

_____

_____

What I can learn (whether this person agrees to help me or not):

_____

_____

_____

_____

In consultation with your own inner observer, please consider the call you have heard and the leap you are about to make. Then do the following exercise.

My call: _____

My Opportunities	My Strengths and Abilities
_____	_____
_____	_____
_____	_____
_____	_____
_____	_____
_____	_____
_____	_____
_____	_____
_____	_____
_____	_____
_____	_____
_____	_____

My Risks

_____
_____
_____
_____
_____
_____
_____
_____
_____
_____
_____

My Allies

_____
_____
_____
_____
_____
_____
_____
_____
_____
_____
_____

My leap: _____

_____

_____

---------------- ❀ ----------------

People say that what we're all seeking is a meaning for life.
I don't think that's what we're really seeking. I think that
what we're seeking is . . . the rapture of being alive.

— JOSEPH CAMPBELL

Life is like arriving late for a movie, having to figure out what was going on without bothering everybody with a lot of questions, and then being unexpectedly called away before you find out how it ends.

— JOSEPH CAMPBELL

Making the Leap

You do not know where your leap will take you. You do not know what effect it will have on the world. It may not even feel like a leap. It may seem more like a push or a fall.

You do not know what the future holds. But here is what you do know: You are not alone. What you are doing matters. This is what you are called to do. You are going to be all right. You are doing your best. Things will somehow work out. In Step Three, you made a decision to turn your will and life over to the care of a Higher Power, and allowed it to restore you to sanity. Now, as you practice the Principle of spirituality and prepare to leap, you place your life in the hands of that Power once again and allow it to guide you into the unknowable future.

In recovery, we express the Principle of spirituality in just this way. With our eyes fixed on a loving Higher Power, we step forward, and then step forward again. And again. We focus not on the difficulties in our way, but on simply taking our next step. And then, one day, we hear the call. We hold out our arms and leap.

Free Fall

The essence of life is free fall. Irrevocable realities thrust themselves on us and suddenly our world moves into a new focus. Over the long context of our lives we see this cycle of challenge evolving into something better. Psychologist Gerald May observed that he, after time, no longer regarded that challenge as bad followed by good. Rather, a new challenge asks us to trust change and the process. Being in free fall over and over leads to a sense of greater purpose. That pain and difficulty are really part of the refining process that calls us to be better people.

Thus we move from the acceptance of irrevocable realities to a heightened awareness, which brings our Inner Observer on board to help make sense of uncertainty. As we continue this cycle we see implicitly the spirituality that comes from a leap of faith. We call these the Free Fall Moments. Our literature is full of examples of the free fall moment. Frodo in *Lord of the Rings* tells Gandalf "that he regretted starting this adventure," which is the same moment as maybe you experienced when starting recovery.

One way to test that idea out for yourself is to create your own Free Fall Profile. Start with the worksheet entitled My Free Fall Moments. Please feel free to continue on another sheet. When done it should be apparent to you that irrevocable realities keep pushing us over the cliff into a struggle which brings us into a stronger, more conscious place.

There are certain strategies that always help in dealing with these moments. Like Harry Potter, who always kept his eye focused on the problem—and he always remembered when he had encountered difficulties in the past but he persevered. Notice what your best strategies are and whether they are easy or difficult for you to do. You also took risks. Look over your free fall moments and select the greatest risks you have taken. Here, too, you will find some easy and some difficult. Finally, distill your key learnings—what do you see as having learned from all of these experiences. Then rate your learnings from difficult to easy in terms of how easy it is to use them.

If you are falling . . . dive.

— JOSEPH CAMPBELL

MY FREE FALL MOMENTS

How they started	How they ended	How I coped
1.		
2.		
3.		
4.		
5.		
6.		

MY FREE FALL PROFILE

My Best Strategies . . .

	Easy				Difficult
1. _____	1	2	3	4	5
2. _____	1	2	3	4	5
3. _____	1	2	3	4	5
4. _____	1	2	3	4	5
5. _____	1	2	3	4	5

My Greatest Risks . . .

	Easy				Difficult
1. _____	1	2	3	4	5
2. _____	1	2	3	4	5
3. _____	1	2	3	4	5
4. _____	1	2	3	4	5
5. _____	1	2	3	4	5

continued

MY FREE FALL PROFILE

My Key Learnings . . .

	Easy				Difficult
1. _____	1	2	3	4	5
2. _____	1	2	3	4	5
3. _____	1	2	3	4	5
4. _____	1	2	3	4	5
5. _____	1	2	3	4	5

I don't know Who—or what—put the question. I don't know when it was put. I don't even remember answering. But at some moment I did answer Yes to Someone—or Something—and from that hour I was certain that existence is meaningful and that, therefore, my life, in self-surrender, had a goal.

— DAG HAMMARSKJOLD

Conversing with Your Inner Addict

As before, find a quiet spot where you can be alone and speak with your inner addict. Read each question below aloud; listen for your inner addict's answer and write it down; then add any other personal reflections you have.

Questions for My Inner Addict about Spirituality

What spiritual and emotional pain are you masking?

_____

_____

_____

_____

_____

_____

_____

_____

_____

When did I make you more important than my life? Remind me of what my spiritual and emotional life was like back then.

_____

_____

_____

_____

_____

_____

_____

_____

_____

_____

The events and crises that brought me to recovery involved
great spiritual and emotional pain. What can you tell me from
your perspective about those events? Have I missed anything
important in those events that is significant to my recovery?

_____

_____

_____

_____

_____

_____

_____

_____

_____

_____

_____

---------------- ❦ ----------------

We must be willing to let go of the life we planned in
order to have the life that is waiting for us.

— JOSEPH CAMPBELL

---❦---

Living a Life of Spirituality

*The big question is whether you are going to be able to
say a hearty yes to your adventure.*

— JOSEPH CAMPBELL

I can practice more spirituality in my life by . . .

Sex

. . . asking my partner to teach me new ways to give pleasure.

. . . telling my partner what I want, even if I'm afraid it will
seem edgy or strange.

. . . not holding back when I feel an urge to scream or sob or
wail.

Add other examples that apply to you.

_____

_____

_____

_____

_____

Money

. . . donating to a cause I have long believed in but never contributed to before.

. . . asking my inner observer, "Will this help me, someone else,
or the world?" when considering a potential purchase.

... reminding myself that no one, including money managers and investment advisors, knows just what the future will bring.

Add other examples that apply to you.

Work

... approaching my work with a spirit of service.

... looking for a different job if my current one won't allow me to be of service in some way.

... learning or trying something that's new, unfamiliar, and challenging.

Add other examples that apply to you.

Intimacy

. . . asking someone I care about, "How can I help?"

. . . allowing someone who is grieving to share his or her grief with me.

. . . serving as an ally for someone I care about.

Add other examples that apply to you.

Lifestyle

. . . regularly consulting my inner observer to get the big picture of the situation.

. . . noticing when I ask myself, "What's in it for me?"—and then also asking, "What will be most helpful?"

. . . changing my plans without regret when I'm needed in an urgent and unexpected situation.

Add other examples that apply to you.

----

*Although not knowing may itself seem like a bad thing,
I am convinced it is one of the great gifts of the dark night
of the soul. To be immersed in mystery can be very
distressing at first, but over time I have found immense relief
in it. It takes the pressure off. I no longer have to worry myself to
death about what I did right or wrong to cause a good or a bad
experience—because there really is no way of knowing.*

— GERALD MAY

. . .

CHAPTER FOUR

Principle Four: Responsibility

{ *Who am I?* }

Step Four.	*Made a searching and fearless moral inventory of ourselves.*

THERE CAN BE NO RECOVERY without responsibility. When we were caught in the web of addiction, we used our emotions to protect us from reality. We guarded our delusions with anger. We masked our pain with fear. We obscured our difficult choices with shame. We blurred our sense of self with sorrow. It's as if we threw a blanket over our life, keeping it dark and confined. When we practiced our addiction, we used our pain to try to shed personal responsibility. We told ourselves that we weren't responsible for our behavior because we'd been abused or abandoned or cheated or because our life sucked.

In recovery, however, we stopped hiding from ourselves. We understand the importance of examining our life, and we accept responsibility for everything in it. We realize that a deeply painful past does not let us off the hook. *Nothing* lets us off the hook. We are always responsible for what we do and decide.

Life Is Not What We Expected

Early in recovery, we discovered that reality was often quite different from our ideas about it. We thought we were in control of our life. We believed we were capable of managing our illness on our own. We imagined that other people were to blame for our situation. We chose delusion and magical thinking over the reality of here and now.

Thankfully, those days are behind us. We have made an ongoing commitment to recovery. We accept that reality is irrevocable, that it is irreconcilable with addiction, and that recovery is often inconvenient because it demands the best from us. Day by day, over and over, we surrender to what is real, and to a process of never-ending discovery and growth. We take responsibility for our life.

Looking back, we see that things rarely turn out precisely the way we thought they would. We *never* know exactly what the future will bring. We still have hopes, dreams, and intentions, but we have learned to hold them lightly. Sometimes the difference between our expectations and reality is vast. When we practiced our addiction, we thought that life without it would be painful and empty. The truth turned out to be exactly the opposite. As our recovery progressed, we began to find pleasure, connection, and joy.

You cannot escape the responsibility of tomorrow by evading it today.

— ABRAHAM LINCOLN

We're in a freefall into the future. We don't know where we're going. Things are changing so fast, and always when you're going through a long tunnel, anxiety comes along. And all you have to do to transform your hell into a paradise is to turn your fall into a voluntary act.

— JOSEPH CAMPBELL

We need to find the courage to say NO to the things and people that are not serving us if we want to rediscover ourselves and live our lives with authenticity.

— BARBARA DE ANGELIS

Your Addiction Tapestry

Many medieval tapestries tell a story in a series of images. Different-colored threads are woven together to create this story, which is typically about a battle, a family, a person, a place, or a marriage. Each human life is also a tapestry that tells a unique story. Your own tapestry is woven from innumerable threads: joy, sorrow, loss, achievement, friendship, love, disappointment, loyalty, betrayal, and a host of other experiences and emotions.

When we practiced our addiction, we wove a tapestry of denial, avoidance, justification, and irresponsibility. It probably also included a grievance: *I became an addict because people did terrible things to me. My parents abused me. My lover abandoned me. My friends failed me. My employer fired me.*

In recovery, however, as our inner observer grows more discerning, it starts to notice flaws in our grievance story. It recognizes how our actions and decisions have contributed to our current situation. We blamed our partner for not being more sexual, but now we see that we did not make ourselves sexually appealing. We resented our boss for failing to promote us, but now we realize that the person who got the promotion has important skills that we failed to develop. Eventually our inner observer realizes that basing our life on grievances doesn't make sense. Our consciousness steadily expands. Our emotional intelligence deepens. We see that regularly reflecting on our life is an ongoing responsibility. We develop mindfulness and discernment not merely as skills, but as *habits*.

For a few minutes, roll out the dusty and damaged tapestry of your old life as an addict. Have your inner observer examine this tapestry carefully. Then answer these questions.

In what ways did my addiction and addictive behavior make my life better?

_____

_____

_____

_____

_____

In what ways did my addiction and addictive behavior make others' lives better? Whose? How?

_____

_____

_____

_____

_____

---

*Look at the word responsibility—"response-ability"—
the ability to choose your response. Highly proactive people
recognize that responsibility. They do not blame circumstances,
conditions, or conditioning for their behavior. Their behavior is
a product of their own conscious choice, based on values, rather
than a product of their conditions, based on feeling.*

— STEPHEN R. COVEY

In what ways did my addiction and addictive behavior make my life worse?

_____

_____

_____

_____

_____

_____

_____

_____

_____

_____

In what ways did my addiction and addictive behavior make other people's lives worse? Whose? How?

_____

_____

_____

_____

_____

_____

_____

_____

_____

_____

What did I take the most pride in back then?

_____

_____

_____

_____

What were the five most important things in my life back then?
What did I most care about?

1. _____

2. _____

3. _____

4. _____

5. _____

In what ways did I seek to avoid responsibility?

Responsibility	*My Avoidance Technique*
_____	_____
_____	_____
_____	_____
_____	_____
_____	_____
_____	_____
_____	_____

Responsibility	*My Avoidance Technique*
_____	_____
_____	_____
_____	_____
_____	_____
_____	_____
_____	_____
_____	_____

In what ways did I use *my addiction itself* as an excuse for irresponsible or hurtful behavior?

_____

_____

_____

_____

_____

_____

What was my personal grievance story?

_____

_____

_____

_____

_____

Which parts of that story were true? Which parts were not?

What was true:

_____

_____

_____

_____

_____

What was not:

_____

_____

_____

_____

_____

How did I see the world and my place in it?

_____

_____

_____

_____

_____

*Acceptance of what has happened is the first step to
overcoming the consequences of any misfortune.*

— WILLIAM JAMES

How did I envision my future—as bright and hopeful, or dark and frightening? (If you went back and forth between competing visions—e.g., positive ones when you were high and grim ones when you were sober—then write about both.)

_____

_____

_____

_____

_____

_____

_____

_____

_____

_____

_____

_____

What were my biggest hopes?

_____

_____

_____

_____

_____

_____

What were my biggest fears?

_____

_____

_____

_____

_____

_____

What things of value did I lose because of my addiction?

_____

_____

_____

_____

_____

_____

_____

_____

_____

_____

_____

_____

_____

Your Recovery Tapestry

In recovery, we weave an entirely new tapestry—one of hope, health, sanity, and serenity—but using the same colors and threads. We include joy, sorrow, loss, achievement, friendship, love, disappointment, loyalty, betrayal—all the same emotions and events as before, plus new ones. We do not leave out or gloss over anything. Yet this tapestry tells an entirely different story.

Have your inner observer carefully examine the tapestry of your life as it is right now, with all its successes, failures, hopes, difficulties, pleasures, and uncertainties. Then answer these questions.

In what ways has recovery made my life better?

We must abandon arrogance and stand in awe. We must recover the sense of the majesty of creation, and the ability to be worshipful in its presence. For I do not doubt that it is only on the condition of humility and reverence before the world that our species will be able to remain in it.

— WENDELL BERRY

In what ways has my recovery made other people's lives better? Whose? How?

_____

_____

_____

_____

_____

_____

_____

In what ways has recovery made my life worse, or more difficult?

_____

_____

_____

_____

_____

In what ways has my recovery made other people's lives worse, or more difficult? Whose? How?

_____

_____

_____

_____

_____

What do I take the most pride in now?

_____

_____

_____

_____

_____

What are the five most important things in my life right now?
What do I most care about?

1. _____

2. _____

3. _____

4. _____

5. _____

What are the five biggest responsibilities that I now accept in my
life? For each one, what is one specific, practical way I regularly
fulfill that responsibility?

Responsibility   *My Responsible Action*

1. _____   _____

2. _____   _____

3. _____   _____

4. _____   _____

5. _____   _____

In what ways do I still sometimes try to avoid responsibility?

Responsibility	My Avoidance Technique
1. _____	_____
2. _____	_____
3. _____	_____
4. _____	_____
5. _____	_____

How do I see the world and my place in it now?

_____

_____

_____

_____

_____

How do I envision my future now? (If you have multiple visions involving multiple possibilities, write about each one.)

_____

_____

_____

_____

_____

_____

_____

What are my biggest hopes?

_____

_____

_____

_____

_____

_____

What are my biggest fears?

_____

_____

_____

_____

_____

What are five specific actions I can *and will* take to face my
fears, live into my hopes, and help create my desired future?

_____

_____

_____

_____

_____

_____

_____

Positive change almost always has a cost or requires us to give up something. (For example, many of us ended relationships with caring friends because they were stuck in their own addictions.) What five specific things that I value will I give up, if necessary, to help create my desired future?

1. _____

   _____

2. _____

   _____

3. _____

   _____

4. _____

   _____

5. _____

   _____

He who experiences the unity of life
sees his own Self in all beings, and all beings
in his own Self, and looks on everything
with an impartial eye.

— BUDDHA

Observing the Inner Observer

In Step Four, as we made a searching and fearless moral inventory of ourselves, we learned that insight is a cornerstone of recovery. As we practice the Fourth Principle of responsibility, we discover that insight is not so much a goal as part of an ongoing mental process.

Responsibility almost always involves action, but it also involves reflection and discernment. Our inner observer monitors all the information that comes into our brain, examines it, and sorts out what is real and valuable from what is not. This requires mental energy, focus, and discipline, which is why good nutrition and adequate sleep are so important to recovery.

In recovery, what begins as a deliberate practice slowly becomes a natural competence. It's much like learning a language. When you begin learning a new language, you need to think through each sentence and mentally translate every word. As you become more fluent, however, some phrases and sentences start to come naturally. Eventually the mental translation disappears and you can think and process information in the new language.

Psychotherapy is similar. In therapy, we examine our life with a therapist in each appointment. In the early stages, however, most of us stop our self-examination soon after the appointment ends and don't pick it up again until the next session. Eventually, though, we begin to see that our greatest growth comes from using the self-examination tools *between* therapy sessions. Over time, this self-examination becomes automatic.

It's the same with religion. As children, most of us were taught to memorize verses from the Scriptures. But we cannot access their profound value unless we carefully examine and meditate on them. The Bible itself tells us this: the words *meditate* and *meditation* appear twenty times—eighteen times in the Old Testament, twice in the New. Yet the word *memorize* does not appear even once.

Psychiatrist Dan Siegel, a leader in the field of interpersonal neurobiology, has spent years studying how our inner observer works.

A fully developed inner observer performs nine related functions at once, from harmonizing the left and right sides of our brain to reflecting on its own role.

Although mindful reflection and the development of an inner observer are essential to recovery, they are not ends in themselves. Day by day, we need to use the insights they give us to make good choices, come to wise decisions, and take concrete, positive action.

Conversing with Your Inner Addict

As your recovery deepens, relying on your inner observer will become more and more of a habit. But this does not mean your inner addict disappears; it still lives within you, and the right combination of conditions can reactivate it. Reach out to your inner addict once again. Answer the questions below, adding further personal reflections if you like.

Questions for Your Inner Addict about Responsibility

If you were to become a healthy part of me, what would you look like? What strengths of mine have you used that I can reclaim?

_____

_____

_____

There are generations yet unborn, whose very lives will be shifted and shaped by the moves you make and the actions you take . . . tonight. And tomorrow. And tomorrow night. And the next. . . . Everything you do, every move you make, matters to all of us.

— ANDY ANDREWS

_____

_____

_____

_____

_____

_____

_____

I would like your help in staying away from extreme living.
What must I commit to in order to have that help? What must
I give up?

_____

_____

_____

_____

_____

_____

_____

_____

_____

_____

What we resist will persist. What have I been unwilling
to acknowledge or accept that encourages you or gives you
energy?

_____

_____

_____

_____

_____

_____

_____

_____

What secrets have I kept from myself by entrusting them
to you?

_____

_____

_____

_____

_____

_____

_____

_____

Living a Life of Responsibility

I am only one, but still I am one. I cannot do everything,
but still I can do something; and because I cannot do everything,
I will not refuse to do something that I can do.

— HELEN KELLER

I can practice more responsibility in my life by . . .

Sex

. . . being honest with a new partner about any STD I may
have and providing adequate protection against it.

. . . discussing and making decisions about birth control with
my partner before having sex.

. . . showing and telling my partner what feels good to me,
rather than expecting my partner to figure it out on his or
her own.

Add other examples that apply to you.

_____

_____

_____

_____

_____

_____

Money

   ... finding the right balance between spending and saving, and being willing to change that balance when necessary.

   ... fully understanding the risks of any investment before I put money into it.

   ... not loaning money to someone I don't trust to repay it, even if that person is a friend or relative.

Add other examples that apply to you.

_____

_____

_____

_____

_____

Work

   ... consistently doing my best at work, even with the parts of my job I don't enjoy.

   ... honestly accounting for my time and expenses.

   ... reporting any unethical or illegal activity, even though I might be punished or fired for it.

Add other examples that apply to you.

_____

_____

_____

_____

_____

Intimacy

. . . telling the truth.

. . . asking for what I want and need, while understanding that I won't always get it.

. . . apologizing and offering amends when I have made a mistake or done something foolish.

Add other examples that apply to you.

_____

_____

_____

_____

_____

Lifestyle

. . . getting enough sleep and eating nutritious food to stay healthy and alert.

. . . keeping a calendar in order to track, monitor, plan, and be on time for appointments.

. . . making good on any promise I make, including any promise to myself.

Add other examples that apply to you.

_____

_____

_____

_____

_____

Do what you can, with what you have, where you are.

— THEODORE ROOSEVELT

· · ·

CHAPTER FIVE

Principle Five: Openness

{ How do I trust? }

Step Five.	*Admitted to God, to ourselves, and to another human being the exact nature of our wrongs.*

MOST OF US SHOW UP at our first Twelve Step meeting with all sorts of trust issues. We trusted people we shouldn't have. We didn't trust people we should have. We didn't tell the truth. We didn't do what we said we'd do. We didn't stay faithful to our partner. We kept secrets. We invaded other people's space. We violated our own value systems. We didn't even know what or whom to trust. In fact, we didn't know *how* to trust and we certainly didn't trust ourselves.

In order to trust, we first need to belong. Yet most practicing addicts don't feel they belong anywhere—except, perhaps, with their addictions or with other addicts.

The Longing to Belong

Before we began our recovery, many of us had little experience of being part of a healthy family, of fitting into a functional community, or of living in a climate of trust. Often, from a very young age, we were denied the opportunity to bond with other people.

I do not believe that sheer suffering teaches. If suffering
alone taught, all the world would be wise, since everyone suffers.
To suffering must be added mourning, understanding, patience,
love, openness and the willingness to remain vulnerable.

— JOSEPH ADDISON

Bonding—or what psychologists also call *attachment*—begins very early in life. Bonding is not about feeding a child, or changing diapers, or making sure a child is entertained (though of course these are important). Bonding occurs when the parent simply holds the child and the two gaze silently in each other's eyes for minutes at a time. The parent is not trying to teach the child something or keep him or her amused. That unblinking gaze is a deep communion— two people being fully present with each other. This experience is vital because it assures the child that he or she has a place in the universe, that the child deserves to be here on the planet, that the child *matters*. Because the child has the full attention of Dad or Mom, the child knows he or she is valued. As a consequence, the child is much more likely to grow up feeling safe, secure, and confident.

Many of us addicts did not have this experience. Our deep human need to bond was thwarted—and we know it. In the depth of our brains, we can feel that we missed out on something. We deeply, and often unconsciously, crave bonding and intimacy. Yet we also have trouble bonding with other people, often because of insufficient bonding experiences when we were small. Instead, we bond with addiction.

A common example is the sex addict who has one new sexual partner after another. The sex may or may not provide physical pleasure, but what the addict really craves are bonding and intimacy. Yet these are precisely what the addict cannot achieve in a stream of casual encounters. With each new sexual experience, the addict hopes to finally feel fulfilled; instead, the addiction worsens.

People who are deprived of bonding as children often grow up feeling unworthy, unconfident, or shameful. These painful feelings can further enable an addiction, as the addict tries to blot out the pain with drinking, drugging, or compulsive behavior.

Becoming Known

In Twelve Step life, all of this changes. When we go to meetings, suddenly we belong. The people in our group understand how we feel, what we've been through, and what we're thinking. As our recovery deepens and we attend more Twelve Step meetings, we begin bonding with other people in the fellowship. Our deep hunger for being part of a group, a clan, a tribe, or a family begins to be fulfilled. We see that we deserve a place in the world and that we are welcome in it. Our Twelve Step group becomes like a family—a family *we* have chosen.

The bonding among people in Twelve Step groups is often profound. Fellow Twelve Steppers often tell me, "This is what I'd always hoped my family would be like. Everybody talks honestly and openly. We laugh together and listen to each other. We don't criticize each other. I've always felt in my bones that this is how it's supposed to be. I'm supposed to have loving, supportive people around me, helping me do my best."

It takes two to speak the truth
one to speak, and another to hear.

— HENRY DAVID THOREAU

*We must come to trust the process of healing enough
to open our heart to the unknown.*

— STEPHEN LEVINE

Finding Your Voice

Bonding is the key to openness. When we have people we can trust and a group where we belong, we can begin to open. We open our minds to new ideas and new ways of seeing the world. We open our hearts to empathy, compassion, and love. And in Step Five, we open our lockbox of secrets and wrongdoings and tell them to someone we trust. This person listens to us and cares about us. It's basic bonding, but adult with adult instead of adult with child.

Something else essential happens in this process. In opening to this person and admitting the exact nature of our wrongs, we make ourselves vulnerable. Our witness learns all about the mistakes we've made, the harm we've caused, and the values and vows we've broken. Yet the listener doesn't disrespect us, or criticize us, or go away upon knowing about our flaws and wrongdoings. Instead, he or she *accepts* us. Our disclosure doesn't end the relationship; it deepens it.

This encounter sends our brain the same message as the silent parent–child gaze. It tells us, *You are redeemable. You do deserve a place on the planet. You belong here.* It is the beginning of our release from feelings of unworthiness and shame. Day by day, we open, we bond, and we heal. It's because of this bonding that many people in Twelve Step groups form lifelong friendships, and many treatment groups continue to meet socially for years after treatment has ended.

Over time, we learn to take this ability to bond out into the world. We also discover that every honest, authentic conversation with another human being—every shared opening—is an opportunity for bonding. Of course, all of this probably seemed a universe away when we first contemplated doing a Fifth Step.

Think back to the first time you did a Fifth Step. Which of the following got in the way? (Check all the items that apply.)

_____ Secrets

_____ Shame

_____ Too much trust in the wrong people

_____ Too little trust in the right people

_____ Too little trust in yourself

_____ _____

In that Fifth Step, we began opening our mouths and speaking the truth. Our voice may have been a hesitant whisper at first. But as we deepened our recovery, told and retold our story, and bonded with more and more people, our voice naturally gained strength, confidence, and volume. This is a wonderful thing, but too much of a good thing can be a problem. As some folks work the Steps and Principles, their voices become too strong, too confident, and too loud. I think of my uncle, who can best be described as stark raving sober. For years he has told almost everyone he meets how wonderfully sober he is. He's addicted to letting the world know about the benefits of sobriety.

Many of us go through this stage in our own recoveries. After a while, though, we become quieter about our sobriety. We realize that our words will never be as profound as our actions and our openness. We speak from our hearts, but not too loudly or too often. We find a middle path between muffling our voice and drowning out others' voices.

When you did your original Fifth Step, how was your voice?

Quiet and hesitant		Confident but subdued		Loud and fervent
1	2	3	4	5

After you were in recovery for a year without relapse, how was your voice when you talked about your recovery?

Quiet and hesitant		Confident but subdued		Loud and fervent
1	2	3	4	5

Has there been a time since then when your voice was not in balance? When was that?

_____

_____

How was your voice back then?

Quiet and hesitant		Confident but subdued		Loud and fervent
1	2	3	4	5

Looking back, why was it out of balance?

_____

_____

_____

Do you sometimes find yourself pulled toward that same lack of balance? If so, under what circumstances or conditions?

_____

_____

_____

_____

What can you reasonably do to limit those circumstances or conditions in the future?

_____

_____

_____

_____

What arrangement can you make with your inner observer to alert you when it sees that you are at risk of losing your vocal balance—or any balance?

_____

_____

_____

_____

When you speak about your recovery today, how is your voice?

Quiet and hesitant   Confident but subdued   Loud and fervent

1   2   3   4   5

Living in Consultation

Openness and bonding go hand in hand. So do openness and problem solving.

When we open up and complete a Fifth Step, we not only bond, but we give another person information about us that enables that person to assist us. Because the person now knows us deeply, he or she can help us solve problems and think things through. This person will also be more likely to catch us in stinking thinking and call us on it. I often use the phrase *living in consultation with others*, which means relying on others' wisdom as well as our own. People are usually far more effective at problem solving in groups than they are as isolated individuals.

Because we are fallible creatures, we human beings often lose perspective on reality. This is true for everyone, but it is especially true for addicts. Our brains are full of ideas, strategies, and approaches that have not worked. Furthermore, we are used to living in isolation and distrust. We need others' experience and wisdom in order to be effective, and we need to open to others in order to rise above isolation and distrust.

As we practice Principle Two, we learn to honestly examine our own perspective and to consult with our Higher Power about what is real and what is illusory. In practicing Principle Five, we also regularly consult with trustworthy people. This means asking for advice and assistance from our sponsor, other Twelve Steppers, trusted friends and family members, and trustworthy experts.

Move out of your comfort zone. You can only grow
if you are willing to feel awkward and
uncomfortable when you try something new.

— BRIAN TRACY

It also means stopping ourselves before consulting with people who *don't* deserve our trust. Usually this means heeding our inner observer's subtle (and sometimes not so subtle) warnings.

Having honest dialogues with others helps us in yet another way. It stimulates our brain by forcing it to think, to make connections, to consider different viewpoints and perspectives, and to ask helpful questions. Each authentic discussion with another person thus stimulates a helpful *internal* discussion among the various parts of our brain.

Your Partners in Openness

No one recovers from addiction alone. Recovery is always a group endeavor.

For a few minutes, mentally review the many people who have helped you in your recovery so far. List them below.

These partners in openness fall into four categories:

- *Witnesses:* folks who witness your recovery with compassion and appreciation.

- *Helpers:* witnesses who also provide personal assistance and guidance.

- *Supporters:* helpers who also stand by you through pain and difficulty.

- *Soul siblings*: supporters who also fully accept you as you are and love you with open hands.

Look back at your list of Partners in Openness. Now place each of your partners in the appropriate category.

Witnesses

_____   _____

_____   _____

_____   _____

_____   _____

_____   _____

Helpers

_____   _____

_____   _____

_____   _____

_____   _____

_____   _____

Supporters

_____   _____

_____   _____

_____   _____

_____   _____

_____   _____

Soul Siblings

_____   _____

_____   _____

_____   _____

_____   _____

_____ ❧ _____

When we honestly ask ourselves which [people] in our lives
mean the most to us, we often find that it is those who, instead
of giving advice, solutions, or cures, have chosen rather to
share our pain and touch our wounds with a warm and tender
hand. The friend who can be silent with us in a moment of despair
or confusion, who can stay with us in an hour of grief and
bereavement, who can tolerate not knowing, not curing, not healing
and face with us the reality of our powerlessness, that is
a friend who cares.

— HENRI NOUWEN

Finding Your Ears

Openness involves listening as well as speaking. In Twelve Step groups, we learn to listen openly, without judgment or cross talk. Although this quickly becomes a habit in meetings, it takes practice and focus to listen as openly in our daily life. This is particularly true when we ask for help. Not everyone will respond by giving us perfect guidance or information. Some comments will be irrelevant or inaccurate. Other responses may be critical, or even offensive.

Practicing Principle Five includes listening without reacting or judging. We learn to stay open even when people say things that hurt or confuse us. The chart on the next page has suggestions for how we can best practice this skill.

When we listen openly to others, we encourage them to open further to us.

Being Open to Others: Your Inner Addict's Advice

In the first column of the following chart, write down an example of a time when you reacted to someone's feedback as described. For the second column, have an internal dialogue with your addict, asking what the addict witnessed as your typical response. For the third column, ask your addict's advice for strategies to make use of feedback that at first seems useless, toxic, or negative.

Whenever people struggle because they have closed off awareness to some aspect of their experience, they need to face that part of themselves to find relief. . . . This is frequently the work that is done in therapy (or even self-help programs, such as Alcoholics Anonymous). . . . The agenda is to explore those aspects of themselves that they have been denying; or have never really known. And, with this exposure, they can begin to experience and understand themselves in new ways; freer to make healthy changes.

— LESLIE BECKER-PHELPS, PH.D.

Type of feedback	My addict witnessed this: (MY TYPICAL RESPONSE IN THIS SITUATION)	My addict suggests this: (WHAT I COULD DO INSTEAD)
A time when I found someone's feedback **personally offensive:**		
A time when I found someone's feedback **inaccurate:**		
A time when I found someone's feedback **irrelevant:**		
A time when I found someone's feedback **unbalanced** (exaggerating the negative; discounting the positive):		

Conversing with Your Inner Addict

Reach out to your inner addict once more. Answer the questions below, adding further personal reflections if you like.

Questions for Your Inner Addict about Openness

Where am I vulnerable? Are there forms or ways in which you appear in my life that I am not facing?

_____

_____

_____

_____

_____

_____

What agreements must we make about feelings? How can I help you when my emotions seem intolerable to you? How can you help me stay with my feelings when they're painful?

_____

_____

_____

_____

_____

_____

_____

_____

How can you help me use my fear to be at my best, rather than to push me toward crisis and despair? Can you help fear become my friend?

_____

_____

_____

_____

_____

_____

What will it take for you to make peace with me? What realities about myself do I have to accept for us to be allies?

_____

_____

_____

_____

_____

_____

_____

_____

_____

_____

———————— ❀ ————————

When we open our heart to our pain,
we make it safe for life to reinhabit our body.

— STEPHEN LEVINE

Living a Life of Openness

If my hands are fully occupied in holding on to something,
I can neither give nor receive.

— DOROTHEE SOLLE

I can practice more openness in my life by . . .

Sex

. . . regularly telling my partner what I appreciate about his or her body.

. . . telling my partner about sexual activities that scare or bother me—and, perhaps, asking my partner to help me move beyond the fear.

. . . surprising my partner with something new, different, and sexy or romantic.

Add other examples that apply to you.

_____

_____

_____

_____

_____

_____

Money

- . . . not keeping information about my finances from my partner.
- . . . looking to my inner observer to help sort out my emotions and values from strictly financial considerations.
- . . . not making assumptions about other people based on the amount of money they have.

Add other examples that apply to you.

Work

- . . . asking for help when I'm having difficulty doing my job well.
- . . . clearly expressing my appreciation for people's help and support.
- . . . willingly sharing my knowledge and experience with coworkers when they ask for it.

Add other examples that apply to you.

Intimacy

... telling people I care about how much they mean to me.

... asking people I trust for their personal advice and guidance.

... allowing someone to tell me about his or her flaws, wrongdoings, or secrets.

Add other examples that apply to you.

Lifestyle

... expressing my opinions forthrightly but not overbearingly.

... being honest about my addiction and recovery, but not broadcasting the details to everyone.

... resisting the temptation to fall into despair or shame when I am turned down for a date, or a bank loan, or something else I wanted.

Add other examples that apply to you.

Part II

❧

Creating Congruence

The second stage of living the Twelve Principles is about creating congruence—fitting the pieces of our life together in a way that works. This stage encompasses Principles Six through Nine: honesty, courage, commitment, and responsiveness.

Congruence naturally involves our relationships with others. We learn to walk our talk, fulfill responsibilities, do what we say we'll do, and be who we claim to be. We harmonize our actions with our speech. We tell others the truth.

A second, equally important form of congruence is internal: We tell *ourselves* the truth. We are clear about our own values and priorities, and we live by them. We work to integrate all aspects of our personality, including those that frighten or worry us. Day by day, we become more of who we want to be.

Our journey of creating congruence leads us deeply into these questions:

- What must improve?

- What risks must I take?

- How am I responsible?

- What is integrity?

We discover the answers to these questions in each new situation. These answers are never static concepts, but actions and decisions that are unique to that moment and context.

As we create congruence, we also discover that we have moved from *being* in recovery to *living* in recovery.

. . .

CHAPTER SIX

Principle Six: Honesty

{ What must improve? }

Step Six.	*Were entirely ready to have God remove all these defects of character.*

WHEN OUR ADDICTION was the center of our world, we lived a double (or triple or quadruple) life. We said one thing and did another. We told different people different stories. We told *ourselves* contradictory stories. And we tried to keep track of it all. But of course we couldn't. No one could. And eventually our world of lies and contradictions imploded.

In contrast, honesty is plain, simple, and clean. Plain because it rarely requires elaboration. Simple because we don't have to keep track of multiple versions. Clean because we don't harm others with it or have to make amends for it.

Honesty with Others

We all know the importance of telling the truth. As we practice the Principle of honesty, we also learn the importance of *living* the truth.

The baobab tree, which grows in Africa and Australia, is often called the upside-down tree because its branches mirror its roots.

What you see at the top of its trunk is much like what grows under-ground. As our recovery deepens, we become more and more like a baobab tree. What we do closely mirrors what we say. We don't keep secrets. What others see is what they get.

Look at the following sample exercise: it shows a baobab tree, seen from both above and below the ground. This tree represents your life. Spend a few minutes thinking on the ways in which your life is not yet transparent and congruent—the ways in which what you say to others differs from what you do. This sample shows a few possible examples.

Then look at the next exercise, which has six empty boxes in each half. For each way your talk and walk don't align, fill in two boxes. In a box among the roots, write what you claim to do or believe. In the box directly above it, among the branches, write what you actually do. For example, you might write *I believe in promptness* in the roots and *I'm often late* in the branches. Circle each box that contains something you feel needs to change. Feel free to add more boxes if you need them.

Most of the time, what we say sounds more honorable than what we actually do. But sometimes it's what we *say* that needs to change. For example, maybe you tell people "I hate exercise," when in fact you take long, brisk walks five times a week. In that case, please reflect on why you give people that false message. Do you see yourself as lazy or undisciplined or physically unfit? Do you mentally compare yourself to your sister the weightlifter? Did you hate exercise years ago but never adjusted your talk to keep up with your walk?

---------------- ❧ ----------------

Recovery calls us to continually work to be more rigorously honest. Rigorous honesty means confronting my shadow and giving up the defensive delusions that guard my wound.

— JOHN BRADSHAW

What I Do and What I Say

Sample exercise

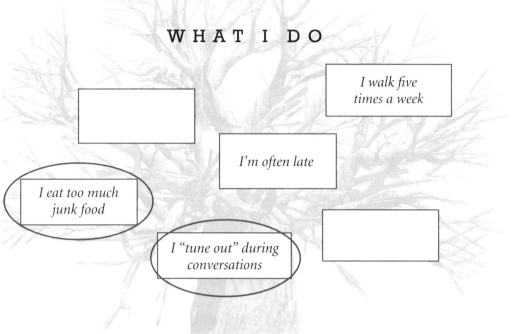

W H A T   I   D O

I walk five
times a week

I'm often late

I eat too much
junk food

I "tune out" during
conversations

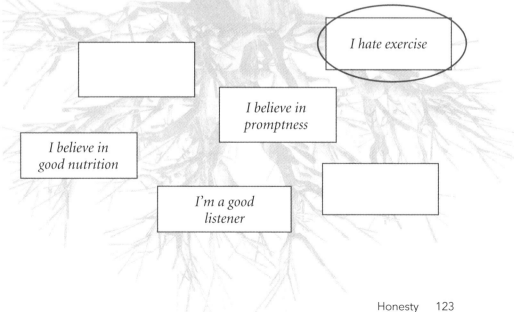

W H A T   I   S A Y

I hate exercise

I believe in
promptness

I believe in
good nutrition

I'm a good
listener

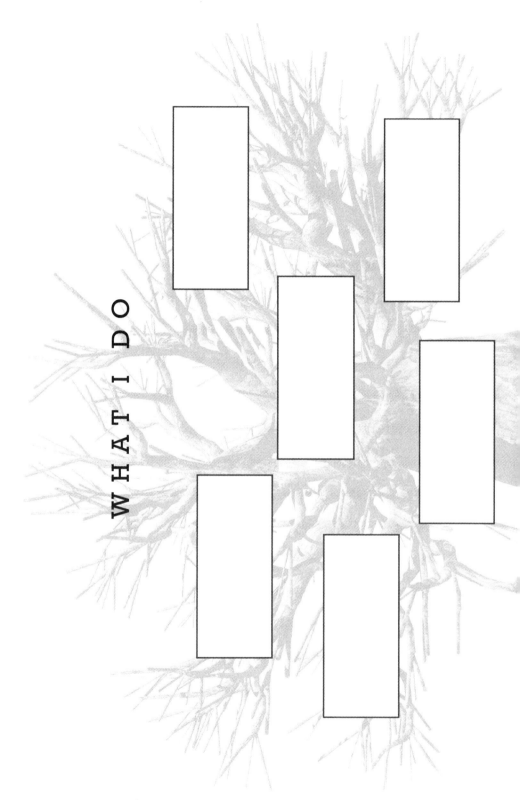

WHAT I DO

WHAT I SAY

Honesty with Yourself

Our recovery requires us to be equally honest with ourselves. As John Bradshaw observes, "Because lying to ourselves (denial) is the core of all addictions, the various Twelve Step groups stress living in a rigorously honest way" ("Some Thoughts on Rigorous Honesty," in the recovery magazine *The Meadowlark,* fall 2005).

When our self-talk doesn't match our actions, the issue almost always involves values—believing in one thing but doing another. We believe in the value of volunteering in our community, yet we spend little time doing it. We value silent retreats, but never go on one. We tell ourselves that we deserve to be happy, but rarely do any of the simple things that bring us joy.

Take a few minutes to reflect on the things you value but don't practice. Then fill in the baobab tree diagram that follows. For each way in which your values and actions don't align, write what you value in a box among the roots; in the box directly above it, among the branches, write what you actually do. For instance, you might write *I value generosity* in the roots and *Last year my income was down, so I gave very little money to charity* in the branches. Add more boxes if you need them.

Here, too, you may discover that it's not always your actions that need to change. Perhaps you see yourself as a highly practical, get-things-done person—yet you find yourself regularly dawdling over breakfast with members of your Twelve Step group. You don't need to cut out the breakfasts or the dawdling (unless it makes you late for work). Instead, you can acknowledge that getting things done *and* simply being with people both have value.

------------------------- ❧ -------------------------

Honesty is the cornerstone of all success, without which confidence and ability to perform shall cease to exist.

— MARY KAY ASH

What I Do and What I Value or Believe

Sample exercise

WHAT I DO

Last year my income
was down, so I gave very
little money to charity.

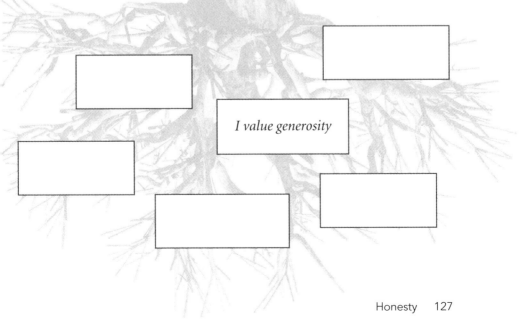

WHAT I VALUE OR BELIEVE

I value generosity

WHAT I DO

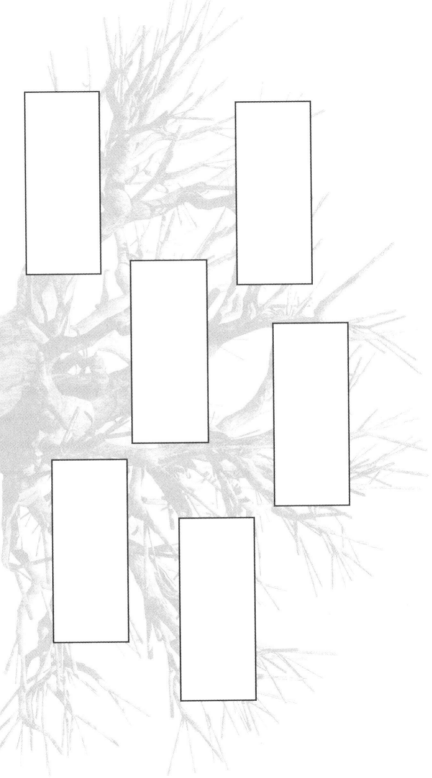

WHAT I VALUE OR BELIEVE

---

*One of the hardest things in this world is to admit
you are wrong. And nothing is more helpful in resolving
a situation than its frank admission.*

— BENJAMIN DISRAELI

Embracing Your Shadow

Being honest with ourselves also involves embracing our shadow—Carl Jung's term for the parts of ourselves that we try to deny or ignore.

In her online column "The Therapist Within," psychologist Gabrielle Gawne-Kelnar described our shadow as "the darker side. The less socially acceptable one . . . the bits you'd rather disown. Or deny. The stuff that might unconsciously drive you in directions that your more public self could feel embarrassed about, shocked over, or even ashamed of. The secret self. . . ."

Everyone has a shadow. It's part of being human. However, each of us has to make a decision about our shadow. We can reach out to it, get to know it, accept it, and learn to work with it—or we can make it our enemy and try to keep it at bay. When we embrace our shadow, it becomes our ally, and it profoundly strengthens our sanity and our recovery. When we treat it as an enemy, however, it forces its way into our life, demanding that it be heard, often creating sabotage or chaos. In a moment of exhaustion or frustration, we suddenly burst out in an embarrassing, over-the-top, out-of-control reaction. If we continue to deny or ignore our shadow, eventually it will start to run our life, and we won't even realize it.

One common reaction to our shadow is to unconsciously project it onto others. Lydia discovers that her teenage son has been looking at pornography online. Furious, she screams at him and takes away his computer for a week, but soon begins visiting some X-rated sites herself. Roger controls his diet very carefully, eating only healthy food. He often wonders aloud why, since people know that sugar is bad for them, they don't just stop eating it. Then, on a beach vacation, he passes a store selling cotton candy and saltwater taffy—his childhood favorites—and binges on both.

When we do a Sixth Step, we become ready to have God remove all our defects of character. As we practice the Sixth Principle, we go deeper; we become ready to let go of our defenses against our own shadow. We understand that this is a necessary part of our healing and recovery, and we know that many treasures await us as we explore this hidden territory.

Exploring and embracing your shadow isn't a one-time activity, like pulling a tooth or tearing down a fence. It's an evolving process that, once begun, will continue throughout your life.

In practicing Principle Six, you'll begin to get to know your shadow. As you practice the remaining six Principles, you and your shadow will steadily become friends and allies.

An Encounter with My Shadow

Think of the last time you did something that was over the top, out of control, or inappropriate, perhaps something that burst out of you unexpectedly. That was your shadow making itself known. Spend a few minutes now mentally reliving that incident from beginning to end.

Make a photocopy of the following questions, then write down the details of the incident you've just recalled in Part 1.

When you finish with Part 1, look over your responses. These will point you directly to a part of your shadow. Gently reach out to that shadow. Don't try to control it, or let it control you; simply examine it with openness and curiosity. This may feel uncomfortable at first. Let yourself stay with this discomfort.

Once you have connected with your shadow, ask it the questions in Part 2 and write down its answers. These will help you to get to know your shadow better, to make peace with it, and to consciously integrate it into your life.

Next, fill in Part 3. The answers to these questions will help you express your shadow in helpful and healthy ways. They will also help your inner observer to notice when your shadow is about to take over—and to de-escalate the situation before that happens.

In the future, each time your shadow appears unexpectedly, make another copy of these pages and fill them in. If you like, you can also reflect on multiple past incidents involving your shadow and fill in multiple copies now. Comparing multiple incidents will help you identify your shadow's behavior patterns and needs.

Part 1: The Past

What I did: _____

_____

_____

_____

_____

When it happened: _____

_____

What went on just before I blew up or acted out: _____

_____

_____

What I felt just before I blew up or acted out: _____

_____

_____

What I thought just before I blew up or acted out: _____

_____

_____

Why I was so upset or excited or provoked; what got
triggered inside me: _____

_____

_____

_____

Part 2: The Present

What do you want or need from me? _____

_____

_____

If I let you do anything you wanted, how would you express
yourself? _____

_____

What are some ways I can let you become part of my life
without you harming anyone? _____

_____

_____

_____

What I need to look at or explore further—perhaps with the help of my sponsor or a therapist: _____

_____

_____

Part 3: Looking to the Future

What happened as a result of my shadow expressing itself:

_____

_____

What I wish I had done instead: _____

_____

What I plan to do next time something similar happens:

_____

_____

What clues will tell my inner observer that I am close to blowing up or acting out in the future: _____

_____

_____

_____

_____

The Strengths in Your Shadow

Your shadow includes all those parts of you that you hide, avoid, or repress. Not all of these are weaknesses or drawbacks. Some may be strengths. Others can *become* strengths if you allow your inner observer to carefully manage them and redirect how you express them. Here are a couple of examples:

- Fredda yearns deeply to give birth and raise a child. But she has no partner and earns too little to support herself and a child. *She could, however, volunteer at a school or daycare center, or provide respite care for kids with developmental disabilities.*

- Kareem was often punished as a child for asking questions and challenging his alcoholic parents' authority. His job as a low-level manager at a call center requires him to steadily improve his center's productivity, but only by using a handful of specific techniques authorized by his superiors. Kareem has plenty of better ideas for making improvements, but his boss refuses to hear them. *Kareem can go over his boss's head, or submit his ideas anonymously, or look for another job.*

Which of your own shadow impulses and desires can become strengths or sources of satisfaction? What can you do to guide them so that they are expressed in a healthy way?

My shadow impulse or desire or source of satisfaction

How I can express it as a strength

_____

_____

_____

_____

_____

_____

My shadow impulse or desire or source of satisfaction	How I can express it as a strength
_____	_____
_____	_____
_____	_____
_____	_____
_____	_____
_____	_____

When Strengths Are Also Liabilities

Sometimes our strengths can also be liabilities—especially if we rely on them too heavily or use them in situations where they simply can't work. Following are a couple of examples.

- When Katarina was young, she faced an unusual number of obstacles. As a result, she learned to come up with fresh and highly creative solutions. Later in life, this talent often enabled her to succeed where others failed. As an adult, this led to a high-paying job with an advertising agency. It also caused her to stay married to a longtime gambling addict until he drove them into bankruptcy. For a decade she came up with fresh, creative solutions to improve the situation, all of which unwittingly supported her husband's addiction and her own co-dependence. Nothing improved until she gave up and made the ordinary, uncreative move of leaving her husband, who entered treatment two weeks later.

- Damon lived by Calvin Coolidge's observation that "Nothing in this world can take the place of persistence. . . . Persistence and determination alone are omnipotent. The slogan 'press on' has solved and always will solve the problems of the human race."

By being persistent and determined, Damon worked his way up from being a salesman for a toy company to being its CEO. When two different Chinese companies flooded the American market with low-priced competitive toys, Damon was unfazed. "We'll weather this," he told his executives and employees. "We built our reputation on high-quality, well-built toys. We don't need to change; we only need to press on. Most of our customers will remain loyal. We'll lose some market share, but we'll stay profitable." Most of his company's customers *did* remain loyal, but then their kids grew up and they stopped buying toys. Meanwhile, new parents flocked to buy the cheap Chinese products instead. Five years later, Damon's company was out of business, and he was out of a job.

What are some of your own skills and talents that have served you well but that have also caused problems when you relied on them too much, or used them in inappropriate contexts?

Every act of dishonesty has at least two victims: the one we think of as the victim, and the perpetrator as well. Each little dishonesty makes another little rotten spot somewhere in the perpetrator's psyche.

— LESLEY CONGER

We tell lies when we are afraid . . . afraid of what we don't know, afraid of what others would think, afraid of what will be found out about us. But every time we tell a lie, the thing that we fear grows stronger.

— TAD WILLIAMS

My skill or talent	How I misapplied it	Results of my misapplication

What Honesty Isn't

None of the Twelve Principles exists in isolation. Honesty that doesn't work in tandem with responsibility or acceptance or awareness can be as harmful as a lie.

Which would you say to your boss: "I have some concerns and questions about your plan" or "Your plan is stupid and doomed to fail"? Which would you say to your partner: "Hon, I think your green sweater will go better with those pants" or "Wow, you have no fashion sense at all, do you"? All four of these statements are honest, but only two demonstrate awareness and acceptance (or any of the other Twelve Principles).

In Twelve Step life, honesty involves much more than just telling the truth. It also includes keeping confidences (but not secrets), respecting and supporting anonymity, maintaining a climate of safety, and not creating harm or unnecessary conflict. We've all known Twelve Steppers who, early in their recoveries, became self-righteous or even brutal. They would often hurt others with their "honesty":

> *"I'm just telling you the truth. It's for your own good."*

> *"I'm not going to enable that kind of behavior."*

> *"Wake up and smell the coffee, Bubba! You're a flaming codependent."*

> *"Lady, you need to see a therapist ASAP."*

These folks may have also gossiped or criticized group members behind their backs. They hadn't yet developed an ethical understanding of what honesty really means. They didn't see that it is part of a larger network of values. In your own efforts to practice the Principle of honesty, have there been times when you have practiced honesty without practicing integrity as well? If so, add this conflict to your baobab tree.

Conversing with Your Inner Addict

Reach out to your inner addict once more. Answer the questions below, adding further personal reflections if you like.

Questions for Your Inner Addict Involving Honesty

> Please tell me honestly and straightforwardly how I learned to be so self-destructive. Now that I am well into recovery, am I still doing any of those self-destructive things?

A lie may take care of the present, but it has no future.

— AUTHOR UNKNOWN

Can you reveal to me how and why I undermined my own efforts and disregarded my most important goals? Am I still doing any of those things now?

_____

_____

_____

_____

_____

_____

_____

_____

How can we partner to limit or end these self-destructive behaviors?

_____

_____

_____

_____

_____

_____

_____

_____

What parts of myself do I still need to reclaim? Are there aspects of myself that I have overlooked or denied in my recovery?

_____

_____

_____

_____

_____

_____

_____

_____

_____

Honesty is the cruelest game of all, because not only can you hurt someone—and hurt them to the bone— you can feel self-righteous about it at the same time.

— DAVE VAN RONK

There is always a way to be honest without being brutal.

— ARTHUR DOBRIN

Living a Life of Honesty

Honesty is the first chapter in the book of wisdom.
— THOMAS JEFFERSON

I can practice more honesty in my life by . . .

Sex

. . . accepting all my sexual desires, including the kinkier ones, and allowing myself to fantasize about them, but not using them to harm anyone.

. . . letting my partner know, without being critical or judgmental, what will make him or her more attractive to me.

. . . letting my partner know what I want as we make love, by moving my partner's hands or giving instructions.

Add other examples that apply to you.

Money

... being realistic about what I can afford, and not living beyond my means.

... being honest and accurate when I do my taxes.

... when I'm undercharged for something, pointing out the error and offering to pay the correct amount.

Add other examples that apply to you.

Work

... not agreeing to do the impossible, but instead negotiating an arrangement that is doable.

... not pretending to have skills, knowledge, or experience that I don't.

... accepting praise and credit for my genuine accomplishments.

Add other examples that apply to you.

Intimacy

. . . saying "I don't know" when I don't know.

. . . stopping and correcting myself as soon as I realize I've exaggerated or misrepresented something.

. . . regularly telling people I care about what I genuinely appreciate about them.

Add other examples that apply to you.

Lifestyle

. . . being straight with myself about the actions that put me in danger of relapse.

. . . letting myself feel all of my selfish and childish impulses— and then setting them aside and doing the next right thing.

. . . telling people if I have an issue or disagreement with them, and then working to resolve it rather than letting it fester.

Add other examples that apply to you.

The truth needs so little rehearsal.

— BARBARA KINGSOLVER

. . .

*If you do not tell the truth about yourself
you cannot tell it about other people.*

—VIRGINIA WOOLF

. . .

CHAPTER SEVEN

Principle Seven: Courage

{ What risks must I take? }

Step Seven.	*Humbly asked Him to remove our shortcomings.*

THE WORD *COURAGE* comes from the Latin word *cor*, which means "heart"—and courage is the heart of recovery. We need courage to say yes. To say no. To say, "I don't know." To try. To fail. To bounce back and try again. To tell the truth. To challenge the status quo. To look foolish. To be wrong. To say, "I'm sorry." To offer amends. To face pain and fear. To risk. To be vulnerable. To live in the unknown. To change. To continue on in the face of resistance.

It took a great deal of courage just to begin recovery. We could have stayed in our addiction until it destroyed us, but we didn't. Instead, we made the courageous decision to face the wreckage we had created and re-engineer our life.

We continue to make courageous decisions day by day as we face our fear and pain. Courage also helps us stay with recovery when we feel like we're not flying at all, but slogging through mud. We're frustrated with how difficult the process is, or how long it takes, or how many obstacles are in our way. We're weary of contending with our shame and sadness and sorrow. In these moments courage reminds us that a life of sanity and serenity is priceless; that we deserve to live such a life; and that, with the help of trustworthy people and our Higher Power, we can create that life.

When we were enmeshed in our addiction, we made a mess of our life—and, almost certainly, others' lives as well. Paradoxically, in recovery we summon the courage to make a mess of things again, but in a positive way. We stop following the rules of our dysfunctional family. We refuse to keep other's secrets (or our own). We end or limit relationships with people who enabled our addiction. We take apart our life, examine every piece of it, and rebuild it from the ground up.

Every time we act courageously, we grow and heal.

—————————— ❦ ——————————

Watch a child learn to walk. They struggle and they fall. Then they bounce back up with a smile on their face and they try again. They are not afraid to fall and somehow intuitively know it is part of the learning process. Failure is a key to learning. It is the fastest route to success because you learn far more from your failures than you do from your successes.

— STEPHEN MILLS

—————————— ❦ ——————————

We gain strength, and courage, and confidence by each experience in which we really stop to look fear in the face.

— ELEANOR ROOSEVELT

We will stumble and fall in the learning process,
but success can only be reached when we are prepared to take
those steps, all of them, even the ones where we fail.

— BOB PROCTOR

Courage and Risk

There is no courage without risk. When we act courageously, we put ourselves on the line for a greater good and make ourselves vulnerable to loss. Instead of arguing with our partner or stalking off, we stay present and loving in the midst of our conflict. Instead of worrying about what people will think, we challenge our coworker when he or she tells a racist joke. Instead of letting someone force us into quickly making an important decision, we insist on taking the time we need. Instead of looking the other way when we see our neighbor hitting a child, we call the police. Instead of following the family rule to never contradict Uncle Nathan, we calmly tell him that we disagree with him and why.

We addicts are not strangers to risk. When we practiced our addictions, we did many enormously risky things. Most of us put other people at risk as well. This wasn't because we were brave; we simply ignored or denied the risks.

In recovery, our approach to risk changes completely. We learn to consider our risks instead of following our impulses. We consult our inner observer, then consciously choose which risks to take. One day at a time, we become both more courageous and more discerning. Although courage is a choice, we do not choose it in isolation. We can ask for help and support from people we trust. We can talk with our sponsor, our therapist, wise experts, or trusted friends or family. We can always ask for the help of our Higher Power.

Your Alignment Map

Courage is where our values meet the world. It means doing the next right thing, even when it's difficult or painful. This always requires mindfulness. When we act out of courage, we know what we're getting into. We have weighed the risks and benefits, held them up against our goals and values, and then made a decision to act. It's the opposite of mindless bravery.

Courage also always has a purpose. We act courageously *for* something: to achieve a goal, fulfill a mission, support a cause or ally, or move toward a vision. One of the most inspiring sections of the AA Big Book, "A Vision for You," offers this depiction of life in recovery.

> Yes, there is a substitute and it is vastly more than that. It is a fellowship in Alcoholics Anonymous. There you will find release from care, boredom and worry. Your imagination will be fired. Life will mean something at last. The most satisfactory years of your existence lie ahead. Thus we find the fellowship, and so will you. . . .
>
> You are going to meet these new friends in your own community. . . . Among them you will make lifelong friends. You will be bound to them with new and wonderful ties, for you will escape disaster together and you will commence shoulder to shoulder your common journey. Then you will know what it means to give of yourself that others may survive and rediscover life. . . .
>
> God will constantly disclose more to you and to us. Ask Him in your morning meditation what you can do each day for the man who is still sick. The answers will come, if your own house is in order. . . . See to it that your relationship with Him is right, and great events will come to pass for you and countless others. This is the Great Fact for us. (Source: *Alcoholics Anonymous*, 4th ed. (New York: Alcoholics Anonymous World Services, 2001), pp. 152–164.)

These words have helped millions of addicts by offering a vision of a saner, happier, more connected life, by creating hope, and by inspiring courage.

As our recovery deepens, we continue to draw courage and hope not only from Twelve Step groups and materials, but from these internal sources:

- *Compelling vision* that provides a clear goal and inspires us to reach it

- *Plan for achieving this vision* by applying the Twelve Steps and Twelve Principles to our life

- *Daily commitment* to the practices, habits, and attitudes that support our recovery and move us toward our vision

- *Purpose;* what we feel called to do in the world (which, at minimum, includes recovering from our addiction)

- *Resolution;* knowledge of the specific things we need to work on, address, or complete in order to achieve our vision

We need all five of these interlocking elements to succeed in our recovery. All five also profoundly support and empower each other.

As part of practicing Principle Seven, complete the following exercise to create a map that shows how these five elements align in your life. Seeing how these fit together will bolster your courage. Your map will also serve as a reminder of what you have achieved and what you still need to work on. As you fill in each section, please don't just write down Twelve Step slogans. Provide concrete details that apply clearly and specifically to your life.

------------ ❦ ------------

One doesn't discover new lands without consenting
to lose sight of the shore for a very long time.

— ANDRE GIDE

My Alignment Map

My Vision

I am working to build a life of sanity, serenity, and success, as I understand success. When I am fully living this life, here is what it will look like:

_____

_____

_____

_____

_____

_____

_____

_____

My Plan

I will grow into the life I envision by completing these phases or action steps:

_____

_____

_____

_____

_____

_____

_____

_____

My Daily Commitments

These are the things I do on a daily (or other regular) basis to help me attain my vision:

To support my physical health

_____

_____

_____

_____

To support my sanity

_____

_____

_____

_____

To support my spiritual health

_____

_____

_____

_____

To support my financial health

_____

_____

_____

_____

To support healthy relationships with others

_____

_____

_____

_____

To support my vision in general

_____

_____

_____

_____

My Purpose

Here are the things I feel called to do before I die:

_____

_____

_____

_____

_____

_____

_____

_____

My Resolution

These are the specific things I still need to work on, address, or resolve in order to achieve my vision—and my specific plans for handling each one:

What I need to do   *When and how I will begin*

_____   _____

_____   _____

_____   _____

_____   _____

_____   _____

_____   _____

_____   _____

_____   _____

_____   _____

_____   _____

My Alignment

If there are items I have listed so far that don't fit together or support each other, I will write them in the following chart. I will also describe how they work against each other, and how I am going to resolve each conflict.

Things that don't fit together	How they work against each other	How I will resolve this conflict
_____ and _____		
_____ and _____		
_____ and _____		
_____ and _____		

My Barriers

If there are things in my life that do not support my vision, my plan, my daily commitments, my purpose, or my planned resolution of unaddressed issues, I will write them below. I will also describe the change I will make to remove or work around each barrier.

What currently gets in the way   *What I will do about it*

_____   _____

_____   _____

_____   _____

_____   _____

_____   _____

_____   _____

_____   _____

_____   _____

_____   _____

_____   _____

_____   _____

_____   _____

The comfort zone is seductive. We all desire comfort. It's human nature. However, too much comfort does not serve us well. An inability to step out of your comfort zone—to challenge yourself, to leave the familiar—will profoundly limit your performance.

— JIM MCCORMICK

Conversing with Your Inner Addict

Reach out to your inner addict and answer the questions below, adding further personal reflections if you like.

Questions for Your Inner Addict Involving Courage

What frightens you the most? What can I do to help allay your fears? What can I do to comfort you?

_____

_____

_____

_____

_____

_____

What do you want me to know that you have never had the courage to tell me before?

_____

_____

_____

_____

_____

_____

————————— ❧ —————————

_. . . living with courage isn't about doing what feels good;
it is the ability to do what is necessary, even when it feels
awkward, unnatural, or downright awful._

— ROBERT E. STAUB II

For all its rewards, sobriety still frightens me in some ways.
What suggestions and encouragement can you give me to help
support my sobriety?

_____

_____

_____

_____

_____

_____

_____

_____

_____

_____

_____

_____

_____

_____

_____

_____

———— ❧ ————

Living a Life of Courage

Courage is the power to let go of the familiar.
— RAYMOND LINDQUIST

I can practice more courage in my life by . . .

Sex

... asking out someone who seems out of my league.

... talking honestly and openly with my partner about a sexual issue or dysfunction I have—and, if appropriate, seeing a doctor or therapist about it.

... firmly but compassionately saying no to sex when my partner tries to pressure or coerce me into it.

Add other examples that apply to you.

Money

- . . . willingly discussing difficult money issues with my partner, while following the guidance of my inner observer in order to stay calm and present.
- . . . saying a polite but firm "no" to a friend or relative who tries to use our relationship to sell me something.
- . . . bargaining for a fair lower price without getting ruffled by a salesperson's pressure tactics.

Add other examples that apply to you.

_____

_____

_____

_____

_____

Work

- . . . reporting unethical activity in my workplace to my boss— or, if necessary, the police.
- . . . taking responsibility when I make a mistake.
- . . . standing up for a coworker who is being scapegoated or treated unfairly.

Add other examples that apply to you.

_____

_____

_____

_____

_____

Intimacy

... honestly telling my partner when I disagree—but without
needing to be right or to get my way.

... standing up to someone in my extended family who tries to
control or shame me.

... saying "I'm sorry; I was wrong" when I discover that I was.

Add other examples that apply to you.

Lifestyle

... telling someone I would like to get closer to that I am
in recovery.

... walking away calmly when someone tries to bait me or
pick a fight with me.

... pressing for redress firmly, persistently, and cool-headedly
when a business cheats or mistreats me.

Add other examples that apply to you.

CHAPTER EIGHT

Principle Eight: Commitment

{ How am I responsible? }

Step Eight.	*Made a list of all persons we had harmed, and became willing to make amends to them all.*

CREATING A SUSTAINABLE recovery involves much more than merely creating sobriety. It's a qualitatively different effort. It's the difference between 2-D and 3-D. Between liking and loving. Between involvement and commitment.

Commitment is absolutely critical to sustaining recovery. Our addiction rewired our brain to sabotage us, to constantly pull us back into our illness. In order to maintain our recovery, we need to *continually* re-engineer our brain—not once, or until we reach a certain goal or threshold, but on an ongoing basis, day by day.

Although commitment is partly about attitude, it is most about what we *do*—how we show up, what responsibilities we shoulder, what decisions we make, and what actions we take to sustain those decisions. Recovery is a team effort that requires multiple commitments: our determination to build a new life, the mindfulness of our inner observer, the help of trustworthy people, and the guidance of our Higher Power.

In Step Eight, we mentally redesigned our relationships with all the people we had harmed. As we live Principle Eight, *we mentally redesign our relationship with recovery.* We no longer see recovery as something we practice; it becomes part of *who we are.* We see that the Principles of recovery are also the Principles of living, and we commit ourselves fully to them.

We addicts already have deep and intimate experience with commitment. When we were caught in our addiction, our commitment to it was nearly absolute. We got very skilled at obtaining whatever substance or experience we were addicted to. We committed great time and energy to planning and organizing these efforts, as well as to covering up our addiction.

Our commitment to recovery needs to be equally thoroughgoing. This means bringing to resolution everything unexamined, undisclosed, unaddressed, or unfinished in our life. It also means asking ourselves, moment after moment, *What is the next right thing I need to do?* As we live the Principles, our commitment to recovery broadens and deepens into a commitment to the world.

The Commitment Equation

As children, we learned from our families how to be responsible and accountable—or else how not to be. Many of us addicts were raised in families that had serious accountability problems. If we grew up in a family with lots of inflexible rules, we learned to get through life in one of three ways:

1. We bought into all the rules and became as inflexible as our parents.

2. We got very good at pretending to follow the rules, while living a secret life in which we did whatever we pleased. (Other family members probably did this, too.)

3. We became very, very rebellious.

In all three cases, we developed an unhealthy view of accountability and commitment.

If we grew up in a family where there were few or no rules, we developed little sense of responsibility or consequences. As adults, we may feel entitled to do whatever we want. We may distrust people and institutions that make or enforce rules. Or we may have swung in the opposite direction, developing a great need for rules, and eventually joining the military, a fundamentalist religious group, or a cult.

One way or the other, many of us addicts were raised in family systems that taught us not to trust rules, or to trust them too much. Meanwhile, when addiction ran our life, we also discovered that we couldn't trust ourselves. This created enormous problems for us, because if we can't trust ourselves, and we assume that other people are basically like us, then we can't really trust anyone. We don't fully trust our partner. We don't fully trust our friends. Our whole life becomes devoid of trust and safety.

You'll recall from chapter 5 that addiction is also an attachment problem. As children, many of us addicts did not have a bonding experience with a loving adult. We grew up craving this bonding in our very cells, yet we lack the skills or experience to bond with others. This creates a cycle of yearning and frustration that either becomes an addiction in itself or drives us to try to soothe ourselves through some compulsive activity. Our injured brains, our accountability issues, and our failure to bond combine to create deep pain and confusion around commitment. As a result, commitment may feel threatening, or suffocating, or beyond our reach.

As we live Principle Eight, however, we slowly unravel this delusion and make commitment our ally.

------------- ✤ -------------

You need to make a commitment, and once you make it,
then life will give you some answers.

— LES BROWN

Commitment and Your Inner Observer

Suppose that you drive the same highway to work every day and always get off at the same exit. One morning you need to deliver a package to a friend who lives three miles further down that highway. Without thinking, out of habit, you automatically take your usual exit. You don't even realize your error until you're halfway down the off-ramp.

Our brain is always creating these kinds of shortcuts for us. It tries to be more efficient, to do more with less energy, so it can free up as much mental bandwidth as possible for other tasks. Much of the time, these shortcuts help us. But when we need to do something different—such as get off the highway three miles later—our mental shortcuts can get in our way.

Most of us have some harmful mental shortcuts as well, such as the ones created by our addictions and our dysfunctional upbringings. For example, when we see a police officer, we may feel an automatic twinge of fear and panic, even though we know the officer's job is to protect and serve us.

In recovery, we work with these mental shortcuts in four ways. First, we train our inner observer to spot them and let us know when they have begun to kick in. Second, we teach our inner observer to tell us when we're in a situation that might trigger an unhealthy shortcut. Third, we learn to stop ourselves from taking certain shortcuts, and to instead act mindfully, based on the particular situation. Fourth, over time we create new, helpful mental shortcuts to replace some of our old unhelpful ones.

Commitment is what transforms a promise into reality. . . .
It is the daily triumph of integrity over skepticism.

— ABRAHAM LINCOLN

This process takes time, effort, and lots of practice—but our recovery requires it. Only with ongoing mindfulness can we make and sustain crucial changes to our brain. Sticking with this process requires commitment. But the process also *creates* commitment: once it starts to yield positive results, it becomes self-reinforcing.

In practicing the first seven Principles, we developed our inner observer into a reliable, mindful presence that monitors and manages all the traffic in our brain. Now, as we live Principle Eight, we also make it responsible for monitoring and managing our daily practices of recovery. These practices differ somewhat from person to person, but they typically include prayer, meditation, personal reflection or writing, and reading Twelve Step materials.

We also give our inner observer the responsibility of managing our *moment-by-moment* practices of recovery. This includes alerting us to:

- Potentially dangerous situations, such as an invitation to a friend's birthday party in a bar, or a Facebook friending request from a former girlfriend.

- Physical or emotional states that make us vulnerable, such as loneliness, disappointment, frustration, exhaustion, or hunger.

- Thoughts or impulses that can get us into trouble, such as a desire to take a walk past the casino, or a brilliant new plan to limit our partner's drinking.

- Mental shortcuts that are inappropriate or potentially damaging.

- Signs that our addiction has reappeared in a new form.

This mutation of one addiction into another is quite common, and represents yet another cunning and baffling aspect of the disease. Even with years of successful recovery under our belt, we can suddenly find ourselves thinking like an addict. Something that had never been a problem for us before—eating, dating, shopping, computer gaming—begins to take on compulsive overtones. These are signs that our addiction has re-emerged with a new focus and is trying to hijack our brain. Our inner observer's careful monitoring can stop this hijacking in its early stages and help us return to the path of recovery.

We also give our inner observer one other important responsibility: helping us create and maintain new, healthy shortcuts and habits. These are often called *unconscious competencies*. They are unconscious because, once we have integrated them into our life, we do them automatically, without thinking. They are competencies because they are always sane and helpful. Common examples include:

- Listening intently without criticism, judgment, or interruption.
- Asking someone who is obviously in distress, "Is something wrong?"
- Asking our Higher Power for help when we need it.
- Being grateful for the good things in our life.
- Asking ourselves *What is needed here? How can I be of service?*

---

*For the wonderful thing about saints is that they were human.
They lost their tempers, got hungry, scolded God, were egotistical
or impatient in their turns, made mistakes and regretted them.
Still they went on doggedly blundering toward heaven.*

— PHYLLIS MCGINLEY

---

*Commitment is healthiest when it's not without
doubt but in spite of doubt.*

— ROLLO MAY

An ounce of performance is worth pounds of promises.

— MAE WEST

Your Character Map

An observation from H. Jackson Brown, author of *Life's Little Instruction Book:* "Our character is what we do when we think no one is looking." It doesn't take a lot of effort or commitment to do what's right when other people are watching. In contrast, commitment requires us to do the next right thing whether people are watching or not. Of course, the reality is that 99 percent of the time, people *are* watching. Secrecy is a delusion. When we practiced our addiction, we discovered that, no matter how hard we worked to keep something secret, someone either already knew it or eventually discovered it.

Furthermore, in Steps Two and Three, we accepted that a Higher Power also watches us—and watches over us. Between other people, our Higher Power, and our inner observer, our actions are never unseen.

Please reflect on the questions below; then write down your answers.

What do I do differently when people are present than when I am alone?

What I do when people are present

_____

_____

_____

_____

_____

What I do when I am alone

_____

_____

_____

_____

_____

_____

Circle each item above that you want or need to change; then list these items again in the following chart. To the right of each item, write what you will do to change it. On the far right, write down who you will ask for help in making this change—e.g., your sponsor, your therapist, trusted friends, family members, your Higher Power, or some combination.

Your Commitment Map

In Step Eight we made a list of all the people we had harmed and made an internal commitment to make amends to them all. As our recovery deepened, we learned that we also need to make amends to _ourselves_, because we are one of the people our addiction harmed the most. Now, in living Principle Eight, we expand this commitment beyond making amends to _doing the next right thing_. Often this means setting something right with another person, even though you did nothing wrong and don't need to make amends. Sometimes it means setting things right with yourself.

Please fill in the chart that follows.

What I want or need to change	How I will begin changing it	Who I will ask for help

What I currently need to set right	Who I need to set it right with	What I will do to set it right

What I need to set right with myself						What I will do to set it right					

Conversing with Your Inner Addict

Reach out to your inner addict and answer the questions below, adding further personal reflections if you like.

Questions for Your Inner Addict Involving Commitment

Am I ready for the commitment to a life of recovery? How do I know I am? What do I need to know in my heart to ensure that I am committed to such a life?

Addiction, achievement, and commitment tap into some of the same processes in the brain. How can you help me to be at my best and avoid my old patterns of self-sabotage?

How can I keep my old addictive behavior from mutating into a new addiction? How can you help me keep that from happening?

_____

_____

_____

_____

_____

_____

_____

_____

_____

_____

You can do what you want to do, accomplish what you want to accomplish, attain any reasonable objective you may have in mind—not all of a sudden, perhaps not in one swift and sweeping act of achievement—but you can do it gradually, day by day and play by play, if you want to do it, if you work to do it, over a sufficiently long period of time.

— WILLIAM E. HOLLER

---⟢ ❀ ⟣---

Living a Life of Commitment

*Stay committed to your decisions, but stay
flexible in your approach.*

— TOM ROBBINS

I can practice more commitment in my life by . . .

Sex

   . . . nurturing my partner and letting my partner nurture me,
sexually and otherwise.

   . . . letting go of delusions about maintaining my relationship
with my partner while having sex with someone else on
the side.

   . . . making sex as satisfying as possible for my partner as well
as for me.

Add other examples that apply to you.

_____

_____

_____

_____

_____

_____

Money

   . . . carefully monitoring and balancing all of my financial accounts each month.

   . . . creating and following a reasonable budget.

   . . . making fair and regular donations to my Twelve Step group.

Add other examples that apply to you.

_____

_____

_____

_____

_____

Work

   . . . consistently making my best efforts.

   . . . keeping up with my field through reading, research, training, etc.

   . . . helping my coworkers excel at their own jobs.

Add other examples that apply to you.

_____

_____

_____

_____

_____

Intimacy

. . . staying connected and open with my partner, even in difficult times and situations.

. . . making sure that my partner and I regularly have fun together, because our commitment to each other includes a commitment to shared pleasure.

. . . being clear about what I want, without trying to coerce or manipulate anyone.

Add other examples that apply to you.

_____

_____

_____

_____

Lifestyle

. . . sticking with a prudent program of exercise and healthy eating—and asking for help when I begin to have trouble.

. . . maintaining a daily practice of prayer, meditation, reflection, journaling, and/or Twelve Step reading.

. . . monitoring and managing my time carefully, so I don't *over* commit myself.

Add other examples that apply to you.

_____

_____

_____

_____

CHAPTER NINE

Principle Nine: Responsiveness

{ *What is integrity?* }

Step Nine.	*Made direct amends to such people wherever possible, except when to do so would injure them or others.*

AS OUR RECOVERY DEEPENS, responsibility grows into responsiveness. Spiritual intelligence unfolds into spiritual integrity. Making amends expands into mending the world.

Step Nine taught us to apologize and make amends whenever we create harm. As we live Principle Nine, we move beyond the personal and the situational. We begin asking ourselves a larger question: *How can I help make things better?* As we go through our day, this question opens into innumerable others: *How can I help my employer succeed? How can I deepen my relationship with my partner? How can I make my community safer? How can I be a better spouse, employee, volunteer, church member, parent, sibling, child, in-law, neighbor, community member, citizen, and steward of the planet? What is the next right thing I need to do?*

In living Principle Nine, we become acutely aware that every one of our actions and decisions has an effect on other people and the world. We begin to bring consciousness and discernment to everything we do. Our focus changes from *me* to *we*.

Our inner observer now assumes a larger role. In addition to monitoring our brain and evaluating each situation, it asks, How can I best be of service? It also prompts us to address difficulties and conflicts sooner rather than later. We deal with things rather than let them languish or fester. In addition, we become more proactive. We think through the likely consequences of each potential course of action—not only its immediate consequences, but what may happen in a week, a month, a year, and ten years. We respond to the future by making wise choices in the present. Day by day, we build integrity.

A key aspect of this integrity is a nimbleness of spirit. One moment we may need to speak up. The next moment we may need to be silent and listen. Responsiveness may prompt us to follow a rule in the morning, enforce a rule in the afternoon, and break a rule (for an honorable reason) in the evening.

It takes less time to do a thing right than it does to explain why you did it wrong.

— HENRY WADSWORTH LONGFELLOW

Remember, if you're headed in the wrong direction, God allows U-turns!

— ALLISON GAPPA BOTTKE

The time is always right to do what is right.

— MARTIN LUTHER KING, JR.

Living in Free Fall

Although we can imagine multiple futures, the actual future is always uncertain and unpredictable. Some of the things we expect to happen don't. Innumerable things we didn't think would happen do. What we embrace as a positive development always creates multiple outcomes—some positive, some negative, some uncertain. Events ripple outward endlessly in all directions.

In his book *Buddhism: Plain and Simple,* Zen teacher Steve Hagen retells the story of an ancient Chinese farmer whose horse ran off. His neighbors expressed their sympathy for his loss—but the next day the horse returned, leading an entire herd. The farmer's son soon broke his leg trying to ride one of the new horses. Then the army passed through and conscripted all the young men except the farmer's injured son. With each new event, the farmer's neighbors told him how lucky or unlucky he was; each time he replied, "Who knows what's good or bad?"

In 2005, I was seriously ill and almost died. Yet I came out of that experience with abilities and perspectives that I am deeply grateful for today. In 2010, my wife died. The loss was so painful that, for a time, I wanted to die, too. I grieve her every day, sometimes every hour. Yet her death has also brought me many unexpected blessings.

We live in free fall. Events cascade around us, and we are presented with one choice after another, each with uncertain outcomes. As we live into Principle Nine, we do our best to stay open and alert. We respond to the challenge of the moment while staying focused on the larger call in our life. In bringing together spiritual nimbleness and a sense of purpose, we create spiritual integrity.

Your Event Cascades

Think back to a deeply painful incident or time. Briefly describe it below.

_____

_____

_____

_____

_____

_____

What did you think would happen in the short term?
In the long term?

Short term: _____

_____

_____

_____

_____

Long term: _____

_____

_____

_____

_____

What actually did happen?

Short term: _____

_____

_____

_____

_____

Long term: _____

_____

_____

_____

Now recall an incident or time when you were especially happy or things were going especially well. Briefly describe it.

_____

_____

_____

_____

_____

_____

———————————— ❀ ————————————

You can't take it back, but you can make it right.

— AUTHOR UNKNOWN

What did you think would happen?

In the short run: _____

_____

_____

_____

_____

In the long run: _____

_____

_____

_____

_____

What actually did happen?

In the short run: _____

_____

_____

_____

_____

In the long run: _____

_____

_____

_____

_____

No and Yes

Mentally revisit a time when you felt called to do something—to act, decide, speak out, take a stand, or make a change—but you chose not to. Describe that situation below.

_____

_____

_____

_____

What did you feel called to do?

_____

_____

What form did the call take? Was it a mental conviction, a bodily feeling, a rising emotion, or something else? Where in your body did you sense it?

_____

_____

Why did you not respond to the call?

_____

_____

What did you do instead?

_____

_____

_____

What happened then?

In the short run: _____

_____

_____

_____

_____

In the long run: _____

_____

_____

_____

_____

Now reflect on another situation where you felt called to act, decide, speak out, take a stand, or make a change—but this time you responded to that call. Describe the situation below.

_____

_____

_____

_____

_____

What did you feel called to do?

_____

_____

What form did the call take? Was it a mental conviction, a bodily feeling, a rising emotion, or something else? Where in your body did you sense it?

_____

_____

How did you respond to the call? What did you do?

_____

_____

_____

What happened then?

In the short run: _____

_____

_____

_____

_____

In the long run: _____

_____

_____

_____

_____

Conversing with Your Inner Addict

Reach out to your inner addict and answer the questions below, adding further personal reflections if you like.

Questions for Your Inner Addict about Responsiveness

Is there something you have been trying to tell me that I have been unwilling to hear or accept? If so, I will do my best to openly listen to it now.

_____

_____

_____

_____

_____

_____

_____

Is there something else I need to do that will make you my ally? If I have been unwilling to do this in the past, I will consider it seriously now, so long as it harms no one.

_____

_____

_____

_____

_____

_____

_____

How can you help me be responsive to practicing addicts?

_____

_____

_____

_____

_____

_____

_____

How can you help me be responsive to other folks in recovery?

_____

_____

_____

_____

_____

_____

_____

———— ✿ ————

You can easily judge the character of a man by how he treats
those who can do nothing for him.

— JAMES D. MILES

Living a Life of Responsiveness

*Live in such a way that you would not be ashamed
to sell your parrot to the town gossip.*

— WILL ROGERS

I can practice more responsiveness in my life by . . .

Sex

. . . letting each sexual encounter evolve, rather than having an agenda for it.

. . . telling my partner what feels good and what doesn't.

. . . letting my relationship with my partner evolve, rather than having an agenda for it.

Add other examples that apply to you.

*Your biggest risk is not the possibility of failing,
it is not trying. Burn this thought into your brain:
The one sure way to guarantee failure to achieve
your dream, is to play it safe.*

— STEPHEN MILLS

Money

   . . . adapting my budget to changes in my income.

   . . . researching and carefully choosing charities, so that my donations have the maximum positive effect.

   . . . maintaining a fund for emergencies—and tapping it without guilt when a genuine emergency arises.

Add other examples that apply to you.

Work

   . . . helping to improve the organization I work for.

   . . . adapting to my coworkers' work styles, rather than demanding that they always adapt to mine.

   . . . knowing when to lead and when to follow—and being willing to do whatever the situation requires.

Add other examples that apply to you.

Intimacy

... acknowledging my partner's emotions without trying to change or fix them.

... accepting that people and relationships change over time.

... being able to give, take, offer, and receive—and knowing when to do each.

Add other examples that apply to you.

Lifestyle

... changing my position on an issue as the situation changes and new information comes to light, rather than clinging to an ideology.

... letting others have the last word.

... adapting my schedule when my commitments change, so that my life stays manageable.

Add other examples that apply to you.

Part III

❧

Growing Vision

The third stage of living the Twelve Principles involves growing our vision into a life of service and meaning. We discover our way, place, and purpose in the world. We learn to trust an unpredictable process of healing and spiritual growth. We get clear about who we are, what we stand for, and what is most important to us, and then we express these through mindful, practical action.

This process calls us to ask ourselves these questions:

- How do I live not knowing outcomes?
- What is the purpose of my life?
- How do I pass it on?

Some answers may come to us as profound flashes of insight, as they did for Paul on the road to Damascus or Buddha under the bodhi tree. Most, however, will show up quietly, like breezes or flowers, as we practice simple, everyday acts of love, wisdom, and service.

. . .

CHAPTER TEN

Principle Ten: Trust

{ How do I live not knowing outcomes? }

Step Ten.	Continued to take personal inventory and when we were wrong promptly admitted it.

RECOVERY TEACHES US—and sometimes forces us—to trust. We learn to trust others. We learn to trust ourselves. We learn to trust an ongoing process of renewal. We give ourselves over to uncertainty, free fall, and the care of a Higher Power.

This is not always a warm and fuzzy experience. Sometimes we trust only because we are desperate or have no other choice. Yet we have reliable maps—the Twelve Steps and the Twelve Principles— and we can always call on our Higher Power for guidance.

At times we'll be anxious or frightened. At times life will seem to be falling apart around us. But we are learning to live with our fear and anxiety, and to practice courage and trust in the face of them. Meanwhile, our inner observer has learned to stay mindful and alert, steering us away from reactivity and focusing us on the next right thing we need to do.

This emphasis on doing is essential. Trust is active, not passive. It emboldens us to speak up, to take a stand, to make decisions, and to move forward into a future we can neither foresee nor control. It prompts us to take one leap of faith after another.

Rebuilding Trust

As we monitor our speech and behavior and practice honesty on a daily basis, we give others more reasons to trust us. Day by day, we continue to rebuild the trust that our addiction destroyed.

This takes time, especially with partners, family members, and close friends, because these are usually the people we hurt and betrayed the most. Because of this, the minute we slip from full integrity even a bit, many of them will notice, admonish us, and pull back. As we establish this practice over time, the important people in our lives will learn that they *can* trust us and will be more forgiving when we slip up.

And we *will* slip occasionally, because living the Principles consistently requires ongoing focus and effort. One day at a time, however, we can become steadily more trustworthy in our dealings with others and with ourselves. We can acknowledge our successes and continue to build on them. And when we do slip, we can ask for help from trustworthy people and from our Higher Power. We can rebuild our trustworthiness in the same way an athlete builds endurance—by working at it every day. In the process, we trust our Higher Power more and more, and we get better at discerning which people to trust and which ones not to. We also rebuild a reservoir of self-trust. Our self-confidence—but not our arrogance—begins to return.

———————— ❀ ————————

Again, you can't connect the dots looking forward; you can only connect them looking backwards. So you have to trust that the dots will somehow connect in your future. You have to trust in something— your gut, destiny, life, karma, whatever. This approach has never let me down, and it has made all the difference in my life.

— STEVE JOBS

From Desperation to Trust

Sometimes we turn to our Higher Power only as a last resort, when everything we have tried has failed and we see that we cannot manage our life or maintain our sanity on our own.

Take a few minutes to reflect on those times in your life when you felt most desperate, hopeless, miserable, or stuck. As you mentally review these situations, pick out three when you made a leap of faith and let yourself trust the unfolding process.

_____

_____

_____

_____

Now please answer the questions below.

Situation 1

What were the circumstances?

_____

_____

_____

When did the event happen? Give the year and the approximate date.

_____

Why was it so difficult or painful?

_____

_____

How did I feel?

_____

_____

What were my fears?

_____

_____

What options did I feel I had?

_____

_____

What was the leap of faith I took?

_____

_____

What were the short-term results of this leap for me and for others?

_____

_____

_____

_____

What were the long-term results for me and for others?

_____

_____

_____

_____

What did I learn or discover as a result of this experience?

_____

_____

_____

_____

Situation 2

What were the circumstances?

_____

_____

When did the event happen? Give the year and the approximate date.

_____

Why was it so difficult or painful?

_____

_____

How did I feel?

_____

_____

What were my fears?

_____

_____

What options did I feel I had?

_____

_____

What was the leap of faith I took?

_____

_____

What were the short-term results of this leap for me and for others?

_____

_____

_____

_____

What were the long-term results for me and for others?

_____

_____

_____

_____

What did I learn or discover as a result of this experience?

_____

_____

_____

_____

Situation 3

What were the circumstances?

When did the event happen? Give the year and the approximate date.

Why was it so difficult or painful?

How did I feel?

What were my fears?

What options did I feel I had?

What was the leap of faith I took?

_____

_____

What were the short-term results of this leap for me and for others?

_____

_____

_____

_____

What were the long-term results for me and for others?

_____

_____

_____

_____

What did I learn or discover as a result of this experience?

_____

_____

_____

_____

Look over your responses. What patterns do you see in your answers? What do they reveal about trusting the unfolding of events? Your Higher Power? Other people? Your inner observer? Yourself?

*We're never so vulnerable than when we
trust someone—but paradoxically, if we cannot
trust, neither can we find love or joy.*

— WALTER ANDERSON

Cascades of Trust

We experience trust in the present, but the actions that build trust can ripple outward for months, years, or centuries. A single act that builds trust can open up the acceptance or empowerment that can change someone's life for the better; that person, in turn, can love and empower hundreds of others. That initial caring act can engender an ongoing cascade of healing events.

Recovery typically creates such a cascade. We may have had a painful and difficult life; we may have struggled for years or decades with addiction; we may have come from a long line of addicts—but the work we do in recovery may spare our children, and their children, and their grandchildren much of the suffering that we endured. Through our own recovery, we may give future generations a chance at a better life.

Or we may not. Nothing is wasted and we can never know what a Higher Power has in store for anyone. Sometimes, in spite of all our efforts and support, our kids may make the same mistakes we did—or worse ones. We also need to remember the lesson of the Chinese farmer: what looks like a blessing can be a problem, and vice versa. Still, we are always wise to envision how our actions and decisions today will affect the next generation, and the generation after that, and the many generations after that. When we take this long view, we are much more likely to help others—and our planet—heal and thrive.

Conversing with Your Inner Addict

Reach out to your inner addict and answer the questions below, adding further personal reflections if you like.

Questions for Your Inner Addict about Trusting

What can I still not trust about you? In what ways can you be cunning and baffling?

_____

_____

_____

_____

As I learn to trust my Higher Power and the unfolding of events, will you try to sabotage that trust? If so, how?

_____

_____

_____

_____

How do I let others know about you without undermining their trust in me?

_____

_____

_____

_____

---◠❦◡---

Living a Life of Trust

For it is mutual trust, even more than mutual interest
that holds human associations together.
— H.L. MENCKEN

I can practice more trust in my life by . . .

Sex

. . . not holding back during orgasm, but giving myself over to
it and trusting my body to complete its natural process.

. . . closing my eyes, lying back, and letting my partner do
whatever he or she wants to me that gives us both pleasure.

. . . telling my partner about some of my sexual fantasies—
and, perhaps, asking my partner to join me in them if my
partner finds them pleasurable as well.

Add other examples that apply to you.

---❦---

To be trusted is a greater compliment than being loved.
— GEORGE MACDONALD

Money

... spending less time worrying about money and more time being grateful for what I have.

... picking investments that reflect the amount of risk I am comfortable with.

... not getting angry at myself when I discover that a reasonable risk I've taken didn't work out.

Add other examples that apply to you.

_____

_____

_____

_____

_____

Work

... not worrying about what my boss and coworkers think of me as long as I'm fulfilling my responsibilities.

... adapting instead of resisting when my duties, job description, or reporting arrangements change.

... staying focused on my core tasks during times of organizational or industry turmoil.

Add other examples that apply to you.

_____

_____

_____

_____

_____

Intimacy

... not holding back emotionally with my partner, or with a dear and trusted friend, but trusting our relationship and letting myself be vulnerable.

... telling my hopes and dreams to people I care about.

... saying calmly to someone I love when I'm angry with that person, "I'm angry at you," and explaining why.

Add other examples that apply to you.

Lifestyle

... taking smart safety precautions, but not worrying excessively about safety to the detriment of enjoying life.

... not becoming upset or reactive when things don't go as planned, and instead adapting or making a new plan.

... asking my Higher Power for help when I am stumped, confused, or at a loss about what to do.

Add other examples that apply to you.

As soon as you trust yourself, you will know how to live.

— JOHANN WOLFGANG VON GOETHE

. . .

CHAPTER ELEVEN

Principle Eleven: Meaning

{ What is the purpose of my life? }

Step Eleven.	*Sought through prayer and meditation to improve our conscious contact with God* as we understood Him, *praying only for knowledge of His will for us and the power to carry that out.*

LIFE IS MESSY. Life has always been messy. It was messy before our addiction began. It was unmanageably messy when we practiced our addiction. Today it is less messy than before, but still messy as hell. It is going to be messy in the future. We often ask ourselves, *When will life stop being such a freaking mess?* We are in recovery, so we already know the answer: never. If we imagine we can control life and make it neat and tidy, we have fallen into stinking thinking, and put ourselves at risk of relapse.

In a 1942 letter, Bill W. wrote, "In God's economy, nothing is wasted." Life is full of loose ends, uncertainty, confusion, and frustration. Yet nothing is wasted or random or pointless. Everything that happens is nourishing compost for our spiritual and emotional growth. It is in the midst of the messiness of life that we often find meaning or, sometimes, that meaning finds us.

Your Peak Moments

For all its messiness, life is also full of beauty, joy, sweetness, and meaning. As we live into the Principles, we learn to accept both life's beauty and its messiness. We become less reactive to difficult or painful situations. We stay anchored in moments of intense joy. Our inner observer reminds us in both cases: *I've seen this before. There's no need to go nuts over it. Just be present with it.* Paradoxically, as we become calmer and less reactive, we also discover—and sometimes rediscover—our passions. The pieces of our life start to fit together. Day by day, our life becomes a public declaration of who we are and what is important to us. We experience ever more meaning and purpose.

To see how the pieces of your own life begin to fit together, spend a few minutes reflecting on those times when you felt most valued or affirmed or connected to the world. As you mentally review these experiences, note the three that were most profound. List them and answer the questions that follow.

Nothing is lost upon a man who is bent upon growth;
nothing is wasted on one who is always preparing for life.
By keeping eyes, mind, and heart open . . .
what he gathers serves him at unexpected moments. . . .

— HAMILTON WRIGHT MABIE

The quest for certainty blocks the search for meaning.
Uncertainty is the very condition to impel man
to unfold his powers.

— ERICH FROMM

Experience 1

What was the situation?

_____

_____

_____

When did this happen? Give the year and the approximate date.

_____

Why was it so meaningful or profound?

_____

_____

_____

How did I feel?

_____

_____

What happened? What did I do?

_____

_____

_____

What options did I feel I had?

_____

_____

What was the leap of faith I took?

_____

_____

What were the short-term results for me and for others?

_____

_____

_____

_____

What were the long-term results for me and for others?

_____

_____

_____

_____

What did I learn or discover as a result of this experience?

_____

_____

_____

_____

———————— ❧ ————————

The world is perfect. It's a mess. It has always been a mess. . . .
Our job is to straighten out our own lives.

— JOSEPH CAMPBELL

Experience 2

What was the situation?

_____

_____

_____

When did this happen? Give the year and the approximate date.

_____

Why was it so meaningful or profound?

_____

_____

_____

How did I feel?

_____

_____

What happened? What did I do?

_____

_____

What options did I feel I had?

_____

_____

_____

What was the leap of faith I took?

_____

_____

What were the short-term results for me and for others?

_____

_____

_____

_____

What were the long-term results for me and for others?

_____

_____

_____

_____

What did I learn or discover as a result of this experience?

_____

_____

_____

_____

_____

*In the last analysis, the individual person is responsible
for living his own life and for "finding himself." If he persists
in shifting his responsibility to somebody else,
he fails to find out the meaning of his own existence.*

— THOMAS MERTON

Experience 3

What was the situation?

_____

_____

_____

When did this happen? Give the year and the approximate date.

_____

Why was it so meaningful or profound?

_____

_____

_____

How did I feel?

_____

_____

What happened? What did I do?

_____

_____

What options did I feel I had?

_____

_____

_____

What was the leap of faith I took?

_____

_____

What were the short-term results for me and for others?

_____

_____

_____

_____

What were the long-term results for me and for others?

_____

_____

_____

_____

What did I learn or discover as a result of this experience?

_____

_____

_____

_____

Look over your answers. What patterns do they reveal? What do they tell you about your life? Your values? Your discernment? Your purpose in the world?

The way you get meaning into your life is to devote yourself to loving others, devote yourself to your community around you, and devote yourself to creating something that gives you purpose and meaning.

— MITCH ALBOM

Your Personal Creed

In religion, a creed is a statement of belief or faith. But each of us also has a personal creed—a set of principles and values by which we live. (For many people, including most practicing addicts, this differs greatly from the creed they *profess* to follow.)

To help you clarify your own personal creed, answer the following questions.

What people and things mean the most to me?

_____

_____

_____

_____

_____

What people and things am I willing to sacrifice for?

_____

_____

_____

_____

_____

What do I spend the most time doing?

_____

_____

_____

_____

_____

_____

What do I wish I spent more time doing?

_____

_____

_____

_____

_____

_____

What are the most important things I have learned about life?

_____

_____

_____

_____

_____

_____

Look over your answers. What do they have in common? What patterns emerge? With these answers in mind, please create your own personal creed and write it below. It can take the form of a list, a paragraph, or a diagram (in which case feel free to use a separate sheet of paper).

The core values and principles I live by are:

_____

_____

_____

_____

_____

_____

_____

_____

_____

_____

_____

_____

_____

_____

_____

_____

---------------- ❀ ----------------

Ultimately, man should not ask what the meaning of his life is,
but rather he must recognize that it is he who is asked.

— VIKTOR FRANKL

Day-By-Day Support

Staying grounded in our beliefs and open to new experiences that give our lives meaning requires more than just good intentions and the right attitude. Each of us also needs a set of daily practices that support our sanity and spiritual health. These practices keep us anchored to the Twelve Steps, the Twelve Principles, and our recovery. They help us focus and strengthen what we have learned. They build our inner observer's mindfulness skills. They reduce our stress and improve our health. They also feel good, because they aren't prescribed for us; each of us gets to decide which practices to include in our life, and how and when to do them. We also get to change or vary them as we wish.

These daily practices include:

- Silent sitting meditation (Vipassana, zazen, Christian meditation, Mindfulness-Based Stress Reduction, etc.)

- Silent walking meditation (in nature, in a labyrinth, etc.)

- Chanting or singing

- Contemplative or liturgical praying

- Spiritual exercising (e.g., those of St. Ignatius or Tibetan Buddhism)

- Quiet reflecting (in nature, in solitude, etc.)

- Practicing yoga

- Mindful reading (on religion, spirituality, or recovery)

- Deep breathing

- Mindful writing (journaling, keeping a spiritual diary, writing Julia Cameron's morning pages, etc.)

- Demonstrating prostrations

- Working with a spiritual card deck

- Doing a mindful ritual of your own design

Add other reflective, meditative, or prayerful practices that have value for you:

- _____

- _____

- _____

Some folks also have an object or image—a candle, book, poster, dream catcher, crystal, stone, etc.—that serves as a personal anchor. This may be the first or last thing they look at each day—or they may keep it in a prominent place where they can see, touch, or hold it when they like.

Here's an adaptation of a simple daily practice from the AA Big Book that many people in Twelve Step programs have adopted.

- In the morning, envision your day as you would like it to proceed, mentally rehearsing it from beginning to end. Ask your Higher Power to direct your thinking and actions.

- At night, silently review the day from beginning to end; note five specific things from the day that you are grateful for; note anything that you wish you had done differently, and make a plan to do it differently next time. Ask yourself: *How was I loving today? How was I caring today? How was I helpful or supportive today?*

In an ideal world, all of us would have ninety minutes a day to spend on these practices—forty-five minutes in the morning and forty-five minutes in the evening—enabling us to begin and end each day in reflection and serenity. If this arrangement isn't possible, then come as close to it as you can. What's most important is regularity—doing something every (or nearly every) day. If ten minutes a day after lunch is all you can manage right now, start with that, and expand your daily practices when you can.

Conversing with Your Inner Addict

Reach out to your inner addict and answer the following questions, adding further personal reflections if you like.

Questions for Your Inner Addict about Meaning

What is most important to you?

_____

_____

_____

_____

_____

_____

_____

_____

What are the most important things you have learned about life?

_____

_____

_____

_____

_____

_____

_____

_____

_____

What are the most important things you have learned
about addiction?

_____

_____

_____

_____

_____

_____

_____

_____

What are the most important things you have learned about me?

_____

_____

_____

_____

_____

_____

_____

_____

_____

———————— ✿ ————————

The least of things with a meaning is worth more in life
than the greatest of things without it.

— CARL JUNG

Living a Life of Meaning

*There is not one big cosmic meaning for all, there is only the
meaning we each give to our life, an individual meaning, an individual
plot, like an individual novel, a book for each person.*

— ANAÏS NIN

I can experience more meaning in my life by . . .

Sex

. . . considering sex an act of giving as well as receiving.

. . . consciously opening my heart to my partner as we make
love.

. . . consciously opening my heart to the whole world as my
partner and I make love.

Add other examples that apply to you.

_____

_____

_____

_____

_____

Meaning is not what you start with, but what you end up with.

— PETER ELBOW

Money

   . . . investing in companies and funds that reflect my values.

   . . . buying products and services that reflect my values.

   . . . shopping at establishments that reflect my values.

Add other examples that apply to you.

_____

_____

_____

_____

_____

Work

   . . . doing work that is of value to me and the world.

   . . . if necessary, looking for a different job or career—one that is of value to me and the world.

   . . . consistently treating my customers, coworkers, subordinates, and superiors with respect and compassion.

Add other examples that apply to you.

_____

_____

_____

_____

_____

The purpose of life is a life of purpose.

— ROBERT BYRNE

Intimacy

... regularly telling my partner how and why he or she is important to me.

... letting my close friends and family know how much they mean to me.

... joining a prayer or meditation group.

Add other examples that apply to you.

_____

_____

_____

_____

_____

Lifestyle

... volunteering at an organization that supports my values.

... taking up an art or craft—singing, writing, dancing, painting, quilting, etc.—that has long appealed to me.

... adopting an abandoned animal from the Humane Society.

Add other examples that apply to you.

_____

_____

_____

_____

_____

CHAPTER TWELVE

Principle Twelve: Generativity

{ How do I pass it on? }

Step Twelve.	*Having had a spiritual awakening as a result of these steps, we tried to carry this message to alcoholics, and to practice these principles in all our affairs.*

GENERATIVITY IS HELPING OTHERS. Giving back. Contributing to society. Making a positive difference. Creating a better world. Leaving a legacy. Guiding and encouraging the next generation—and the many generations thereafter. The word *generativity* was coined by psychologist Erik Erikson. It is the seventh (middle adulthood, ages 40–65) of his eight stages of human development. Erikson observed that as we mature, we must make a choice: either we live in a generative way or we become spiritually and emotionally stagnant. Although generativity has multiple dimensions, all of them involve using our experience, insight, and passion to help others. Having found meaning in our life, we offer the best of ourselves to the world. We live intentionally, mindfully, and generously.

The Call of the Moment

In every situation, generativity prompts us to ask—and answer—these questions: How do I pass on my gifts to others? How do I use my skills, knowledge, possessions, and relationships to make things better?

The answers to these questions are always practical and down to earth. We help push our neighbor's car out of a snow bank. We baby-sit for our daughter and son-in-law. We organize a demonstration against corruption in our city's government. We stay late at work to help a client or coworker in distress. We mentor a new hire, or a fifth grader. We leave the beach or picnic ground cleaner than we found it. We conserve water. We volunteer at the local animal shelter. We plant trees along the river to prevent erosion. We take in our homeless nephew. We lovingly toss him out again when we discover that, despite our clear prohibition, he has continued to take and deal drugs in our home. In each case, we answer the call of the moment.

Every moment and every interaction is an opportunity for generativity. Even if we are simply sitting alone in a room, we open our heart and send loving kindness into the world. But if we also see that the floor is dusty, we sweep it. And if we suddenly conceive of a much better way to sweep floors, we share our idea with the world.

Generativity takes innumerable forms. Giving. Nurturing. Supporting. Mentoring. Leading. Guiding. Advising. Speaking out. Confronting. Creating. Following. Listening. Bearing witness. Standing up for a person or a cause. Simply being present with someone as he or she experiences great pain or joy or difficulty. Generativity can even take the form of mindfully doing nothing. Instead of shouting "no!," we stand back and let our four-year-old grandson step onto the thin ice of our backyard pond. We watch silently as he breaks through and falls to his knees in nine inches of water. He screams, gets up, and runs back to us. Only then do we gather him in our arms, kiss him, and carry him inside.

Generativity is always intentional. Our inner observer monitors the situation, discerns how we can make a positive difference, and prompts us to do the next right thing. If it sees that a detailed strategy is needed, it asks for help from other parts of the brain. And if it sees that there's nothing we need to do right now, it stays silent and watchful.

One thing I know; the only ones among you who will be really happy are those who will have sought and found how to serve.

— ALBERT SCHWEITZER

Help others and give something back. I guarantee you will discover that while public service improves the lives and the world around you, its greatest reward is the enrichment and new meaning it will bring your own life.

— ARNOLD SCHWARZENEGGER

Be the change you want to see in the world.

— MOHANDAS GANDHI

Contributing by Doing and Being

Take a few minutes to recall moments or periods in your life when you contributed to the world in a meaningful way or created a profound blessing in someone's life. As you mentally review these experiences, note the ones that were particularly helpful or significant. Of these, please pick two in which you took an active role and did something important. In a phrase, describe each of these two experiences below.

1. _____

_____

_____

_____

2. _____

_____

_____

_____

Now pick an experience that involved *being* rather than *doing*—one where you bore witness to someone or stood by someone in a moment of conflict, pain, or difficulty. Describe this experience here.

3. _____

_____

_____

_____

Now please answer the following questions.

Experience 1: Doing

What was the situation?

_____

_____

_____

When did this happen? Give the year and the approximate date.

_____

What did I do?

_____

_____

What were the short-term results?

_____

_____

_____

_____

What were the long-term results?

_____

_____

_____

_____

Experience 2: Doing

What was the situation?

_____

_____

_____

When did this happen? Give the year and the approximate date.

_____

What did I do?

_____

_____

_____

What were the short-term results?

_____

_____

_____

_____

What were the long-term results?

_____

_____

_____

_____

Experience 3: Being

What was the situation?

_____

_____

_____

When did this happen? Give the year and the approximate date.

_____

How was I helpful?

_____

_____

_____

What were the short-term results?

_____

_____

_____

_____

What were the long-term results?

_____

_____

_____

_____

Playing Our Music

Although generativity focuses on giving, there is a receiving aspect to it as well. Through generativity we connect with others, as well as to our own talents and to what gives us meaning and purpose. Oliver Wendell Holmes observed, "Most of us go to our graves with our music still inside us." Generativity encourages us to play that music for as long as we are willing and able.

One of the stories in Andy Andrews's book *The Noticer* involves an aging widow named Willow who is waiting to die. She is healthy and financially stable, but she feels she has nothing left to live for or offer the world. Then she encounters the book's protagonist, who laughs gently at the notion that she has outlived her usefulness. "Who gave you permission," he asks her, "to decide that you had nothing more to do, nothing more to offer?" He reels off a long list of people who made a difference in their eighth and ninth decades of life. By the time they are done talking, Willow has moved from stagnation and hopelessness into the beginnings of generativity. She realizes that she still has much to give to the world and plenty of time left to give it.

------------------------- ❧ -------------------------

There are certain things that are fundamental to human fulfillment. The essence of these needs is captured in the phrase "to live, to love, to learn, to leave a legacy."... [Th]e need to leave a legacy is our spiritual need to have a sense of meaning, purpose, personal congruence, and contribution.

— STEPHEN R. COVEY

Long-Term Generativity

Generativity prompts us to think not only of the present, but of the future—including the far future. As we share our gifts with the world, we keep in mind the generations to come: our children, grandchildren, great-grandchildren, and great-great-grandchildren. We realize that the efforts we make today don't just benefit us; they leave a legacy.

Spend a few minutes thinking about the spiritual legacy you want to leave behind. Then ask yourself the following questions and write your answers in the chart that follows.

- What insights, skills, and attitudes do I want to pass on to others before I die?

- To whom do I want to pass them?

- What must I do next to begin or advance this process?

- When am I going to do it? (Don't write "soon" or "ASAP"; provide a specific date.)

Generativity and Discernment

Generosity of spirit is a core aspect of generativity—but so are mindfulness and discernment. We give because we have things worth sharing and a willingness to share them. But generativity prompts us to not share anything that will hamper others' growth or limit their ability to live the Twelve Principles.

For example, giving lots of money to our kids can damage them. As a therapist, I see a lot of emotionally stunted trust-fund kids—and similarly stunted adults. They inherited enough money that they don't have to work, take risks, or push themselves. As a result, they face few big challenges in life—and they receive few opportunities to rise to them. Instead of growing spiritually and emotionally, they often become self-involved and depressed. They're much like a butterfly emerging from a cocoon. It has to struggle to force its way out. Yet that very struggle is what strengthens its wings so that it is able to fly. If we were to help the butterfly escape by slitting a hole in the cocoon, it would fall out, be too weak to fly, and die.

Insight, skill, or attitude	Who I want to pass it on to	What I need to do next	When I will do it
1.			
2.			
3.			
4.			
5.			

Your Vision Timeline

In this and the previous two chapters, you mentally revisited nine spiritually significant moments, incidents, or periods of your life. In chapter 10, it was the three times in your life when you felt the most desperate and made a leap of faith, letting yourself trust the unfolding process. In chapter 11 it was the three times you felt most valued or affirmed or connected to the world. And in this chapter, you listed three ways, two by doing and one by being, that you contributed to the world in a meaningful way or created a profound blessing in someone's life.

Look back at those pages now and copy the descriptions and dates you listed below.

Event   **Date**

1. _____   _____

2. _____   _____

3. _____   _____

4. _____   _____

5. _____   _____

6. _____   _____

7. _____   _____

8. _____   _____

9. _____   _____

If you want to build for one year from now, grow wheat.
If you want to build for ten years from now, grow trees.
If you want to build for one hundred years from now, grow people.

— CHINESE PROVERB

Now list these events chronologically, from the earliest to the most recent. For each event, also create a one-to-three-word name (for example, Jenny's Graduation or South Carolina Trip). Write these below.

Event   **Date**

1. _____   _____

2. _____   _____

3. _____   _____

4. _____   _____

5. _____   _____

6. _____   _____

7. _____   _____

8. _____   _____

9. _____   _____

Next, create a timeline that begins with the earliest event and ends in the present. Place the other eight events in the appropriate spots on this timeline.

Name of event #1   **Today**

_____

Look over this timeline for a few minutes. What does it reveal about your contributions to the world? About the ways in which you can serve others? About your purpose in life or your role in the world? About what you still need to do? Does a pattern or progression emerge? Does anything else important reveal itself? Write your thoughts and responses below.

_____

_____

_____

_____

_____

_____

_____

_____

_____

_____

_____

_____

_____

_____

_____

_____

------------------------------ ❦ ------------------------------

One generation plants the trees; another gets the shade.

—CHINESE PROVERB

Conversing with Your Inner Addict

Reach out to your inner addict and answer the following questions, adding further personal reflections if you like.

Questions for Your Inner Addict about Generativity

Do you have a legacy of learnings to leave for others through me? What wisdom can you offer to begin to make amends for the harm we caused?

_____

_____

_____

_____

_____

_____

_____

Is there anything else we need to look at or work through together?

_____

_____

_____

_____

_____

_____

_____

_____

Now that you no longer control my life, do you have any wishes, hopes, or advice for me?

_____

_____

_____

_____

_____

_____

_____

_____

We can't all leave a prestigious background or lots of money to visit our children, but we can leave them a legacy of love.

— NAOMI RHODE

Do all the good you can, in all the ways you can, to all the souls you can, in every place you can, at all the times you can, as long as you ever can.

— JOHN WESLEY

Living a Life of Generativity

No matter what age you are, or what your circumstances might be, you are special, and you still have something unique to offer.

— BARBARA DE ANGELIS

I can practice more generativity in my life by . . .

Sex

. . . staying faithful to my partner—and expecting my partner to remain faithful as well.

. . . answering my young kids' questions about sex honestly, straightforwardly, and in a way they can understand.

. . . refusing to condone or keep secrets about friends' and family members' infidelity.

Add other examples that apply to you.

_____

_____

_____

_____

_____

In every community there is work to be done. In every nation, there are wounds to heal. In every heart there is the power to do it.

— MARIANNE WILLIAMSON

Money

... structuring financial gifts and bequests so they do the most good—and don't hamper anyone's growth.

... saving enough for my retirement that I am not a financial burden to my partner or children.

... teaching my kids about saving, investing, and managing money.

Add other examples that apply to you.

_____

_____

_____

_____

_____

Work

... mentoring less-experienced employees.

... coordinating a Take Our Daughters and Sons to Work® day at my workplace—and strongly encouraging my own kids to participate.

... using my contacts to help talented family members and friends find jobs and internships.

Add other examples that apply to you.

_____

_____

_____

_____

_____

Intimacy

> ... writing a living will or health care directive, so my loved ones know exactly what to do if I am unable to make my own medical decisions.

> ... being a Big Brother or Big Sister for a child in my town.

> ... providing a temporary home for a foster child or foreign exchange student.

Add other examples that apply to you.

_____

_____

_____

_____

_____

Lifestyle

> ... learning CPR, first aid, water lifesaving, and other skills that enable me to be helpful in an emergency.

> ... coaching a kids' sports team.

> ... sponsoring an impoverished child or family overseas.

Add other examples that apply to you.

_____

_____

_____

_____

_____

Part IV

✿

Living Into the Principles

The Twelve Principles, like the Twelve Steps, are eminently practical as well as inspirational. They consistently put our feet to the ground.

The chapters that follow bring this idea into focus. They offer field-tested recipes for working the Twelve Principles and living a life of sanity and service. The first of these chapters provides a down-to-earth process for monitoring, managing, and strengthening your recovery. The second applies the Principles to the art and skill of problem solving. Together, these chapters will help you navigate life's perfect messiness with greater wisdom, compassion, and discernment.

CHAPTER THIRTEEN

The Twelve Principles Day by Day

SOBRIETY AND RECOVERY are never accidental. They are gifts we continue to receive only if we maintain and strengthen them. The Three Circles are an effective, easy-to-use tool for tracking and reinforcing your own recovery. Here is how it works.

Imagine three circles, one inside the other, like a bull's-eye. The outermost circle is your safe zone. It includes all the things you can do to strengthen your recovery and live the Twelve Principles in all your affairs. The innermost circle is your addiction zone. It contains all your old addictive behaviors—the things you simply *can't* do anymore. The middle circle is your danger zone. It contains those things you need to avoid because they can easily pull you back into your addiction.

The middle circle is where your inner observer does some of its most important work. As it monitors your brain and your situation, it notices when a middle-circle activity or situation appears. It then sends you a warning and steers you back toward your outer circle as quickly as possible. If that doesn't work, it prompts you to call your sponsor, your therapist, or someone else who can help you regain your footing. (See diagram on next page.)

For example, Joachim is a recovering sex addict who has been faithful to his girlfriend Vicki for the past three years. He maintains his sobriety by not picking up people in bars, not hiring prostitutes, not arranging hookups online, not going to strip clubs, and not using pornography. These activities all appear in Joachim's inner circle.

The Three Circles

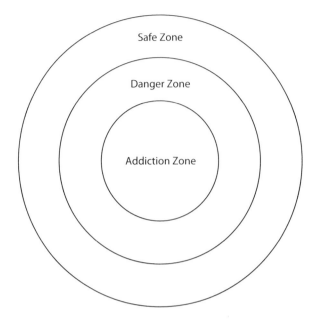

If he does any one of them, it's a slip; if he has multiple slips over a brief period, he has relapsed.

Joachim's outer circle includes going to Sex Addicts Anonymous meetings twice weekly, reading Twelve Step literature for fifteen to thirty minutes a day, and meeting once a month with his sponsor. It also includes activities that promote his physical, emotional, and spiritual health: working out twice weekly, walking in the park for half an hour a day, seeing his therapist once a month, meditating every morning, and going to at least one prayer service a week. Because giving to the world, sharing our gifts, and spending time in meaningful activities are intrinsic to our recovery, Joachim's outer circle also includes volunteering at the neighborhood food pantry, serving as a scoutmaster, and learning to play the cello.

Joachim's middle circle holds activities that aren't a problem for most people, but are definitely problems for Joachim, because they can easily trigger his addiction. These include walking past adult bookstores; driving through areas where hookers walk the streets; looking at online posts for hookups; attending bachelor parties; reading interviews with porn stars; spending time with his brother, who is a practicing sex addict; or scanning websites that sell sex toys. (Using these toys with Vicki is not a problem, but in order to support his sobriety, he and Vicki have agreed that she will shop for them.) Joachim knows that he needs to avoid these activities—and that if he starts doing any of them, he is in danger of relapse and needs to quickly contact his sponsor or therapist, or go to a Twelve Step meeting. Joachim's middle circle also contains stressful activities and situations that have nothing to do with his addiction, but nevertheless make him vulnerable to it. These include getting less than eight hours of sleep, delaying a meal by more than two hours, working more than six days in a row or more than ten hours a day, neglecting to meditate for two days in a row, visiting Vicki's parents for more than two to three hours, and attending any gathering of his extended family.

The Three Circles look two-dimensional, but in fact they are like a funnel or drain. The closer we get to the center, the more likely we are to get sucked back down into our addiction; the closer we get to the outer edge, the more level the ground is beneath our feet, and the easier it is to stay anchored in our recovery.

Start at the Bottom

Make a photocopy of the blank Three Circles diagram. If you have more than one addiction, make a copy for each one. However, please don't work with more than one addiction per day. Find a quiet, comfortable spot where you can reflect undisturbed for at least an hour. Bring a pen, paper (or your computer), and your blank Three Circles diagram with you. The list you're about to create will take you at least half an hour, and the process will be painful at times—so relax and take it easy. If you need to stop partway through and come back to this exercise later, that's fine. Have mercy on yourself.

Mentally review the arc of your addiction, from its beginnings until the day your long-term sobriety began. As you do this mental review, make a written note for each event or experience that was especially painful, harmful, destructive, or self-destructive. You don't need to describe each event in detail; just give it a name or brief description such as *Bonnie's auto accident* or *When the dogs got loose.* Don't stop when you reach ten items. Keep reviewing your past until you get to your sobriety date. Let your list be as long as it needs to be.

Once you've created this list, look it over for a few minutes. Then pick out what you would rate as the ten worst moments of your addiction. Note these below.

1. _____

2. _____

3. _____

4. _____

5. _____

6. _____

7. _____

8. _____

9. _____

10. _____

If you have difficulty narrowing your list to ten items, then twelve or fifteen are fine—but get as close to ten as you can.

Your "No Way" List

Take out your blank Three Circles diagram and look through the list you just created. For each event on the list, think of all the things you did that were addictive, harmful, or both. These are the things you simply cannot do again. Write these in your center circle to create your abstinence list.

Your Addiction Boundaries

Look at your Ten Worst Moments list again, but shift your focus a bit. Identify all the decisions, actions, and activities that *led to* your addictive behavior. Most of these will not be harmful in and of themselves; but they nevertheless pulled you down a slippery slope to trouble. These will include mistakes, misjudgments, things that teased and tempted you, and things that stressed you out. Write these in your middle circle. These are your addiction boundaries.

Your Best and Healthiest Self

In your outer circle, list the things you can do on a regular basis that will bolster your recovery and make a positive difference in the world. These should be clear, specific, down-to-earth, and realistic—no fantasies or pipe dreams, please. These actions and activities can include things you already do, things you have considered doing but not yet begun, new things that come to mind now, and things suggested to you by others (your partner, your sponsor, your therapist, etc.).

List as many of these as you like, writing outside the outer circle if necessary. But do list *at least two* that embody or support each of the Twelve Principles—a minimum of twenty-four in all. Coming up with two items for each of the Twelve Principles may take some time. If you need to stop and return to this exercise later in order to complete it, that's fine.

When your diagram is complete, review it with your sponsor or therapist and ask for comments and suggestions. Then consult your Three Circles regularly to monitor, deepen, and inspire your recovery.

Looking Forward

I encourage you to update your Three Circles as your circumstances change and your recovery warrants. At least twice a year, sit down with this diagram and see if any changes appear to be necessary. A word of caution, however: don't make *any* change without running it past your Twelve Step group, sponsor, or therapist. Remember, addiction can be cunning and baffling. It always has the potential to reappear in a new guise, catch you at a vulnerable moment, and hijack the Three Circle process.

CHAPTER FOURTEEN

Problem Solving with the Twelve Principles

At the end of each Twelve Step meeting, we usually feel safe, sane, and serene. Then we leave the building and the messiness of the world hits us like a pie in the face. The Twelve Principles can help us clean up our own messes and avoid making new ones, but they won't clean up the world's inherent messiness. Instead, the Principles help us to heal, love, find meaning, and be of service in the midst of life's ongoing mess. One way the Principles do this is by providing a practical recipe for solving problems. This chapter lays out that recipe step by step.

Observing Your Situation

Think of a personal problem you've been wrestling with. This shouldn't be something that's trivial or that has an obvious solution (your car's brakes are failing, so get them fixed). The problem should be big enough to significantly affect your life. It should also be personal (for example, your mother is dying or your brother has been arrested) rather than general (for example, the country has gone to war or a tsunami has hit the city). Some other examples:

- You learn that your daughter and son-in-law, who have a nine-year-old son, are leaving each other—and you believe the problem is mostly your daughter.

- You discover that your aorta is 50 percent blocked. You need to change your health habits and lifestyle *now*.

- You find out that your spouse of twenty-six years was married and divorced long before the two of you met.
- Your partner dies.
- Your child is diagnosed with leukemia.
- Your company downsizes and, at age fifty-eight, you lose your job as a mid-level manager.
- Your home is seriously damaged by a hurricane.

Now, briefly describe your problem below.

_____

_____

_____

_____

_____

What has kept you from resolving the problem?

_____

_____

_____

_____

_____

What situations from your past remind you of your problem? Recall those situations and fill in the chart that follows.

Situation	How it is similar to my current problem	What I did that helped	What I did that didn't help	What I learned

Applying the Principles

Now that you've connected your current problem to your past experience and learning, you're ready to connect them with the Twelve Principles. Because each Principle reflects and reinforces the other eleven, the Twelve Principles can be represented as a wheel.

The Twelve Principles

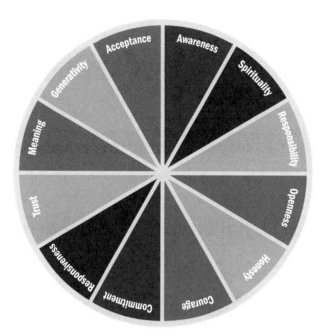

Look over this wheel and reflect on what you've learned about each Principle. If you like, revisit earlier portions of this book. Then list by name the Principle or Principles you feel can best help you address your problem.

_____

_____

_____

Your Range of Possibilities

Now consider your options. In the blanks below, list every course of action you can think of that might address your problem or make your situation better. Reflecting on the Principles you've chosen will help you find as many options as possible. For now, don't think about whether any action is reasonable or easy or practical. You're simply brainstorming. Sometimes the most unconventional or off-the-wall idea is the one that actually works; in other cases, the idea may be unworkable, but leads to another idea that creates a solution.

My options:

1. _____

2. _____

3. _____

4. _____

5. _____

6. _____

7. _____

8. _____

If more than eight options occur to you, write them on a separate sheet of paper.

Enlisting the Help of Others

Before making any important decision, it's wise to consult with someone you trust—or two such people, or three, or as many as you need. You will ask some of these people for ideas, guidance, suggestions, and support; you will ask others for direct, hands-on assistance. It's always wise to ask your Higher Power for help as well.

In the end, you may not follow others' recommendations. They may not even make recommendations at all; they may say, "I don't know what to do; I'm sorry." They may deeply disagree with you, or with each other. Yet they will almost always bring something valuable to the process: a new perspective, an important question or consideration, or a suggestion of someone else to consult.

Consulting someone you trust also enables you to tell the full, honest story of your problem to someone—and for that story to be heard. Whom you approach for help depends on your contacts, your situation, and your needs. Depending on your problem, your most helpful allies might include a professional (a roofer, a mechanic, a therapist, a physician, an exterminator, etc.), your sponsor, a good friend, a neighbor, a coworker, or someone from your church whose family member has the same problem as yours, and so on. Whomever you approach, however, they should be people you trust, people who will tell you the truth. It's always tempting to ask for help from people who are warm and compassionate and understanding—but if you can't trust them to be completely honest with you, they may do you more harm than good.

In the spaces on the next page, list all the people you believe can help you address your problem and how they can help.

Name	How this person can help
_____	_____
_____	_____
_____	_____
_____	_____
_____	_____
_____	_____
_____	_____
_____	_____
_____	_____
_____	_____
_____	_____
_____	_____
_____	_____
_____	_____
_____	_____
_____	_____
_____	_____
_____	_____

When your list is complete, rank the people numerically based on how helpful you feel they can be. Then go down your list and begin asking for assistance. You get to decide whether to talk with each person one-to-one, to have a group conversation, or both. As you discuss your problem, show your answers to the questions in this chapter. This will help these people to guide you—and to alert you if they see that you're headed in a dangerous direction.

Your Solutions List

Now you're ready to take action.

Based on your answers and your consultations with others, create a list of all the solutions you have decided to try, *in the order in which you will try them.* If you plan to try two or more solutions at once, draw a single circle around them. For each solution, write down every specific, concrete step you will take to implement it, as well as when you will do it (i.e., *next week* or *tomorrow evening* or *when Clarissa gets back*, not *soon* or *ASAP*).

Give your first solution enough time to work. If it does not adequately resolve your problem, move on to the next solution. Keep going down your list until the problem is addressed or you are out of options. Keep in mind that a solution may satisfactorily address a problem without bringing about the precise resolution you wanted or expected. For example, you may not convince your daughter and son-in-law to stay together—but they may end up on cordial terms, living half a block apart (and five blocks from you), amicably sharing custody of their son. You may not clear up your aortic blockage in a year, but you may develop and stick to an exercise program that steadily improves your health. After accepting your spouse's apology for keeping the first marriage secret, you may decide that you made too big a deal of your spouse's lack of disclosure, and offer an apology of your own.

Solution	The steps I will take	When I will take each step
1.	a. b. c.	
2.	a. b. c.	
3.	a. b. c.	
4.	a. b. c.	
5.	a. b. c.	

Into the Future

Once you've addressed your problem, one final part of this process remains: preventing similar problems in the future. Look over everything you've written in this chapter, the solutions you applied, and the results of those solutions. Then reflect on how you can head off similar problems in the future. Write your thoughts below.

I can prevent similar problems in the future by:

1. _____

_____

2. _____

_____

3. _____

_____

4. _____

_____

5. _____

_____

6. _____

_____

The Final Exam . . .
about the Questions of Life

A GREAT STORY about Albert Einstein came from his own gradu-ate students in physics. Second-year students were surprised to see that the questions on their final exam were the same as the questions on the first-year final. When asked about it, Einstein responded that, of course, the questions are always the same ones. Further, what he expected was that their answers would change. So in essence he measured their growth by their improved responses and saw that the world presented the same basic questions.

So it is with the Principles. Each Principle inherently is about the basic life issues that we will encounter over and over again. All of us must face them, not once, but many times. The essence of these life issues can be captured in a question. Recognizing the question dramatically increases our ability to respond. Assembled together they provide a unique road map for living life well.

The answers reside in the Principles. And like Einstein's students, each time we encounter them, they teach certain life lessons. With time and focus, the emotional topography becomes more easily recognized, allowing access to history, strategies, and personal wisdom. In short, our answers get better. However, if we fail to learn, the lessons become more difficult. Also the lessons can get more challenging even if we do learn them. The intent of it all is how we are refined by the struggle as individuals, and perhaps, as a species. So it is important to see that the Twelve Steps teach critical principles to these enduring questions. The notion that we "graduate" or finish is delusional for they will reappear again. When they do, you will note how "this time" the mess seems to be uniquely positioned to test you—and not always in fun ways. Sometimes they are fun. Always they seem to have personal ironies based on our past answers.

To help you with this perspective as well as create a way for you to measure your own progress, we close with a final exam. You may want to wait a while to let everything you've done in this book sink in and to see how you're able to apply the Principles in your life today. If you've been using a notebook or journal to do the exercises in this book, then use it to do this exam. If not, start a journal now that you can keep around to continue this exercise over time.

When you're ready, look back over your answers to the questions in this book and reflect on each Principle from one through twelve, write down your thoughts on how you think your life will change, or is already changing, by applying these Principles in your ongoing recovery. Date this entry and put your journal or notebook aside until you feel it's time to refresh your memory or renew your recovery and do the same exercise again and date that entry. That way you can measure your progress over time when circumstances prompt you to return to this book. Perhaps at some point you will point out to a sponsee or friend or family member that the current issue being faced is really the question (one of our twelve). And perhaps they will ask how you know. You can always respond by saying, "It is on the final exam."

Thank you for making this journey. May you continue to practice the Twelve Principles in all your affairs.

❧

Appendix A

Twelve Steps with Twelve Principles

Step	Principle
Step One We admitted we were powerless over alcohol—that our lives had become unmanageable.	Principle One Acceptance
Step Two Came to believe that a Power greater than ourselves could restore us to sanity.	Principle Two Awareness
Step Three Made a decision to turn our will and our lives over to the care of God *as we understood Him.*	Principle Three Spirituality
Step Four Made a searching and fearless moral inventory of ourselves.	Principle Four Responsibility
Step Five Admitted to God, to ourselves, and to another human being the exact nature of our wrongs.	Principle Five Openness
Step Six Were entirely ready to have God remove all these defects of character.	Principle Six Honesty
Step Seven Humbly asked Him to remove our shortcomings.	Principle Seven Courage

continued

Step	Principle
Step Eight Made a list of all persons we had harmed, and became willing to make amends to them all.	Principle Eight Commitment
Step Nine Made direct amends to such people wherever possible, except when to do so would injure them or others.	Principle Nine Responsiveness
Step Ten Continued to take personal inventory and when we were wrong promptly admitted it.	Principle Ten Trust
Step Eleven Sought through prayer and meditation to improve our conscious contact with God *as we understood Him,* praying only for knowledge of His will for us and the power to carry that out.	Principle Eleven Meaning
Step Twelve Having had a spiritual awakening as a result of these steps, we tried to carry this message to alcoholics, and to practice these principles in all our affairs.	Principle Twelve Generativity

Appendix B

Twelve Step Support Group Information

Adult Children Anonymous/
Adult Children of Alcoholics
adultchildren.org
> Box 3216
> Torrance, CA 90510
> 562-595-7831

Al-Anon
al-anon.org
> 1600 Corporate Landing Parkway
> Virginia Beach, VA 23454
> 757-563-1600
> Fax: 757-563-1655
> E-mail: wso@al-anon.org

Alateen
al-anon.alateen.org
> 1600 Corporate Landing Parkway
> Virginia Beach, VA 23454
> 757-563-1600
> Fax: 757-563-1655
> E-mail: wso@al-anon.org

Alcoholics Anonymous
aa.org
> Box 459
> New York, NY 10163
> 212-870-3400

Anorexics and Bulimics Anonymous
aba12steps.org
> Box 125
> Edmonton, AB T5J 2G9 Canada
> 780-318-6355
> E-mail: aba@shawbiz.ca

Chapter 9—Couples in Recovery
Anonymous
chapter9-nyc.org
> Box 245
> New York, NY 10159
> 212-946-1874;
> 888-799-6463 (toll free)
> E-mail: info@chapter9couplesin
> recovery.org

Cocaine Anonymous
ca.org
> Box 492000
> Los Angeles, CA 90049-8000
> *also*
> 21720 S. Wilmington Ave.,
> Suite 304
> Long Beach, CA 90810-1641
> 310-559-5833
> Fax: 310-559-2554
> E-mail: cawso@ca.org

Co-Anon and Co-Ateen (for relatives and friends of cocaine addicts)
Co-anon.org
  Box 12722
  Tucson, AZ 85732-2722
  520-513-5028;
  800-898-9985 (toll free)
  E-mail: info@co-anon.org

COSA (for coaddicts whose lives have been affected by other people's compulsive sexual behavior)
cosa-recovery.org
  Box 79908
  Houston, TX 77279-9908
  866-899-2672
  E-mail: info@cosa-recovery.org

Co-Dependents Anonymous (CoDA)
coda.org
  Box 33577
  Phoenix, AZ 85067-3577
  602-277-7991;
  888-444-2359 (toll free, English);
  888-444-2379 (toll free, Spanish)
  E-mail: outreach@coda.org

Compulsive Eaters Anonymous/HOW
ceahow.org
  5500 East Atherton St., Suite 227-B
  Long Beach, CA 90815-4017
  562-342-9344
  Fax: 562-342-9345
  E-mail: gso@ceahow.org

Crystal Meth Anonymous
crystalmeth.org
  4470 W. Sunset Blvd, Suite 107,
  Box 555
  Los Angeles, CA 90027-6302
  213-488-4455

Debtors Anonymous
debtorsanonymous.org
  Box 920888
  Needham, MA 02492-0009
  781-453-2743;
  800-421-2383 (toll free)
  Fax: 781-453-2745
  E-mail: office@debtorsanonymous.org

Double Trouble in Recovery
(for people with addictions and mental illnesses)
scshare.com/downloads/DTR_Brochure.pdf (downloadable brochure)
youtube.com/watch?v=Akma7v9Ik_A (Hazelden "Double Trouble in Recovery" video)
  803-727-4631

Dual Recovery Anonymous
(for people with addictions and mental illnesses)
draonline.org
  Box 8107
  Prairie Village, KS 66208
  913-991-2703
  E-mail: draws@draonline.org

Eating Addictions Anonymous
eatingaddictionsanonymous.org
  Box 8151
  Silver Spring, MD 20907-8151
  202-882-6528
  E-mail: eaagso@eatingaddictions anonymous.org

Eating Disorders Anonymous
eatingdisordersanonymous.org
  Box 55876
  Phoenix, AZ 85078-5876
  E-mail: info@eatingdisorders anonymous.org

Emotions Anonymous
(for people working toward recovery
from emotional difficulties)
emotionsanonymous.org
> Box 4245
> St. Paul, MN 55104-0245
> 651-647-9712
> Fax: 651-647-1593

Families Anonymous
(for anyone in recovery from the effects
of a loved one's addiction)
familiesanonymous.org
> 701 Lee Street, Suite 670
> Des Plaines, IL 60016-4508
> Phone: 847-294-5877;
> 800-736-9805 (toll free)
> Fax: 847-294-5837

Food Addicts in Recovery Anonymous
foodaddicts.org
> 400 W. Cummings Park, Suite 1700
> Woburn, MA 01801
> 781-932-6300
> E-mail: office@foodaddicts.org

Gamblers Anonymous
gamblersanonymous.org
> Box 17173
> Los Angeles, CA 90017
> 626-960-3500 (office);
> 888-424-3577 (helpline)
> Fax: 626-960-3501
> E-mail: isomain@
gamblersanonymous.org

Heroin Anonymous
heroin-anonymous.org
> 5025 N. Central Avenue, #587
> Phoenix, AZ 85012

Incest Survivors Anonymous
lafn.org/medical/isa/home.html
> Box 17245
> Long Beach, CA 90807-7245
> 562-428-5599

Marijuana Anonymous
marijuana-anonymous.org
> Box 7807
> Torrance, CA 90504
> 800-766-6779
> E-mail:
> office@marijuana-anonymous.org

Nar-Anon (for relatives and friends
of people with drug addictions)
nar-anon.org
> 22527 Crenshaw Blvd., Suite 200B
> Torrance, CA 90505
> 310-534-8188;
> 800-477-6291 (toll free)

Narcotics Anonymous
na.org
> Box 9999
> Van Nuys, CA 91409
> 818-773-9999
> Fax: 818-700-0700

Nicotine Anonymous
nicotine-anonymous.org
> 6333 E. Mockingbird, #147-817
> Dallas, TX 75214
> 877-879-6422
> E-mail:
> info@nicotine-anonymous.org

Online Gamers Anonymous
olganon.org
> 104 Miller Lane
> Harrisburg, PA 17110
> 612-245-1115

Overeaters Anonymous
oa.org
Box 44020
Rio Rancho, NM 87174-4020
505-891-2664
Fax: 505-891-4320

Pills Anonymous
pillsanonymous.org

Recovering Couples Anonymous
recovering-couples.org
Box 11029
Oakland, CA 94611
781-794-1456;
877-663-2317 (toll free)

S-Anon and S-Ateen
(for people who have been affected
by others' sexual behavior)
sanon.org
Box 111242
Nashville, TN 37222-1242
615-833-3152;
800-210-8141 (toll free)
E-mail: sanon@sanon.org

Self Sabotagers Anonymous/
Misery Addicts Anonymous
miseryaddicts.org

Sex Addicts Anonymous
sexaa.org
Box 70949
Houston, TX 77270
713-869-4902;
800-477-8191 (toll free)
E-mail: info@saa-recovery.org

Sex and Love Addicts Anonymous
slaafws.org

Sexaholics Anonymous
sa.org
Box 3565
Brentwood, TN 37024
615-370-6062;
866-424-8777 (toll free)
Fax: 615-370-0882
E-mail: saico@sa.org

Sexual Compulsives Anonymous
sca-recovery.org
Box 1585, Old Chelsea Station
New York, NY 10011
212-606-3778;
800-977-4325 (toll free)

Sexual Recovery Anonymous
sexualrecovery.org
Box 178
New York, NY 10276
E-mail: info@sexualrecovery.org

Spenders Anonymous
spenders.org

Survivors of Incest Anonymous
siawso.org
Box 190
Benson, MD 21018-9998
410-893-3322

Workaholics Anonymous
workaholics-anonymous.org
Box 289
Menlo Park, CA 94026-0289
510-273-9253
E-mail:
wso@workaholics-anonymous.org

www.12step.org
(for anyone dealing with any addictive
or dysfunctional behavior)

Appendix C

Recovery Resources from
Dr. Patrick Carnes and Associates

Gentle Path Press provides a wide range of recovery resources, including books, workbooks, audios, videos, posters, and the *Recovery Start Kit*, which provides guidance, support, and inspiration for the first 130 days of recovery. Many of these resources are written or cowritten by Patrick Carnes. The Gentle Path site also offers FAQs on sexual addiction and sexual anorexia, links to recovery fellowships, and a tool to help locate a therapist.

> **gentlepath.com**
> Box 3172
> Carefree, AZ 85377
> Toll Free: 800-708-1796
> Office: 480-488-0150, 800-708-1796 (toll free)
> E-mail: info@gentlepath.com

International Institute for Trauma and Addiction Professionals (IITAP) promotes professional training and knowledge of sexual addiction and related disorders. Sex addiction affects the lives of millions of people worldwide, and practicing therapists are on the front lines, treating this epidemic. IITAP offers three certifications to addiction treatment professionals: Certified Sex Addiction Therapist (CSAT), Certified Multiple Addiction Therapist (CMAT), and Associate Sex Addiction Therapist (ASAT). Its website, iitap.com, is the leading online resource for sex addiction professionals. It includes a wide range of useful resources for mental health professionals, including articles, newsletters, links, upcoming events and trainings, an online forum, and an online tool for locating a sex addiction therapist.

iitap.com
Box 2112
Carefree, AZ 85377
480-575-6853; 866-575-6853 (toll free)
Fax: 480-595-4753
E-mail: info@iitap.com

Patrickcarnes.com provides detailed information on upcoming talks, presentations, workshops, and other events featuring Patrick Carnes and his colleagues.

Recoveryzone.com offers a regular newsletter on recovery, plus several free anonymous assessments: a sexual addiction screening test, a sexual addiction risk assessment, and a partner sexuality survey.

Sexhelp.com offers a wealth of free resources, information, and inspiration for sex addicts and people in recovery from sexual addiction. The site includes on-line tests, articles, FAQs, and news of upcoming events, plus links to Twelve Step fellowships, recovery centers, and other helpful organizations.

Sexhelpworkshops.com provides details on many upcoming workshops, programs, and trainings offered by Patrick Carnes and his colleagues.

Sexualaddictiontherapists.com offers a variety of articles and videos on sexual addiction, a free sexual addiction screening test, and links to helpful resources of all types.

Bibliography

Alcoholics Anonymous World Services, Inc. *Alcoholics Anonymous,* 4th ed. New York, 2002.

Alcoholics Anonymous World Services, Inc. *Twelve Steps and Twelve Traditions.* New York, 2002.

Amen, Daniel G. *Making a Good Brain Great.* New York: Three Rivers Press, 2006.

Andrews, Andy. *The Noticer.* Nashville, TN: Thomas Nelson, 2009.

Beattie, Melody. *Beyond Codependency: And Getting Better All the Time.* Center City, MN: Hazelden, 1989.

Becker, Ernest. *The Denial of Death.* New York: The Free Press, 1997.

Black, Claudia. *Double Duty: Help for the Adult Child.* New York: Ballantine Books, 1990.

Bradshaw, John. *Bradshaw On: The Family: A New Way of Creating Solid Self-Esteem,* rev. ed. Deerfield Beach, FL: Health Communications, Inc. 1990.

Bradshaw, John. *Creating Love: The Next Great Stage of Growth.* New York: Bantam Books, 1994.

Bradshaw, John. *Healing the Shame That Binds You,* rev. ed. Deerfield Beach, FL: Health Communications, 2005.

Brown, H. Jackson. *Life's Little Instruction Book.* Nashville, TN: Rutledge Hill Press, 1991.

Cameron, Julia. *The Complete Artist's Way: Creativity as a Spiritual Practice.* New York: Tarcher, 2007.

Campbell, Joseph. *The Hero with a Thousand Faces,* 3rd ed. Novato, CA: New World Library, 2008.

Carnes, Patrick. *Don't Call It Love: Recovery from Sexual Addiction.* New York: Bantam Books, 1992.

Carnes, Patrick. *Facing the Shadow, Second Edition: Starting Sexual and Relationship Recovery: A Gentle Path to Beginning Recovery from Sex Addiction.* Carefree, AZ: Gentle Path Press, 2006.

Carnes, Patrick. *Out of the Shadows: Understanding Sexual Addiction,* 3rd ed. Center City, MN: Hazelden, 2001.

Carnes, Patrick. *Recovery Zone, Volume 1: Making Changes That Last: The Internal Tasks.* Carefree, AZ: Gentle Path Press, 2009.

Carnes, Patrick. *Sexual Anorexia: Overcoming Sexual Self-Hatred.* Center City, MN: Hazelden, 1997.

Carnes, Patrick, Stefanie Carnes, and John Bailey. *Facing Addiction: Starting Recovery from Alcohol and Drugs.* Carefree, AZ: Gentle Path Press, 2011.

Carnes, Patrick, Debra Laaser, and Mark Laaser. *Open Hearts: Renewing Relationships with Recovery, Romance, and Reality.* Carefree, AZ: Gentle Path Press, 1999.

Chodron, Pema. *Comfortable with Uncertainty: 108 Teachings on Cultivating Fearlessness and Compassion.* Boston: Shambhala, 2003.

Chodron, Pema. *The Places That Scare You: A Guide to Fearlessness in Difficult Times.* Boston: Shambhala, 2005.

Chodron, Pema. *Taking the Leap: Freeing Ourselves from Old Habits and Fears.* Boston: Shambhala, 2010.

Chodron, Pema. *When Things Fall Apart: Heart Advice for Difficult Times.* Boston: Shambhala, 2002.

Coelho, Paulo. *The Alchemist.* New York: HarperCollins, 2006.

Coelho, Paulo. *Warrior of the Light.* San Francisco: HarperOne, 2004.

Covey, Stephen R. *The Seven Habits of Highly Effective People,* rev. ed. New York: Free Press, 2004.

Csikszentmihalyi, Mihaly. *Flow: The Psychology of Optimal Experience.* New York: HarperCollins, 2008.

Frankl, Viktor. *Man's Search for Meaning.* Boston: Beacon Press, 2006.

Geller, Anne. *Restore Your Life: A Living Plan for Sober People.* New York: Bantam Books, 1992.

Geringer Woititz, Janet. *Adult Children of Alcoholics,* exp. ed. Deerfield Beach, FL: Health Communications, 1990.

Goleman, Daniel. *The Brain and Emotional Intelligence: New Insights.* Northampton, MA: More Than Sound, 2011.

Goleman, Daniel. *Emotional Intelligence.* New York: Bloomsbury, 2010.

Goleman, Daniel. *The Meditative Mind: The Varieties of Meditative Experience.* New York: Tarcher, 1996.

Goleman, Daniel. *Social Intelligence: The New Science of Human Relationships.* New York: Bantam, 2007.

Grant, Ginger. *Re-Visioning the Way We Work: A Heroic Journey.* Lincoln, NE: iUniverse, 2005.

Hammarskjold, Dag. *Markings.* New York: Vintage, 2006.

Hirschfield, Jerry, Ph.D. *The Twelve Steps for Everyone . . . Who Really Wants Them,* rev. ed. Center City, MN: Hazelden, 1987.

Kabat-Zinn, Jon. *Coming to Our Senses: Healing Ourselves and the World Through Mindfulness.* New York: Hyperion, 2006.

Kabat-Zinn, Jon. *Wherever You Go, There You Are.* New York: Hyperion, 2005.

Kurtz, Ernest and Katherine Ketcham. *The Spirituality of Imperfection: Story-telling and the Search for Meaning.* New York: Bantam, 1993.

Kurtzweil, Ray and Terry Grossman. *Transcend: Nine Steps to Living Well Forever.* New York: Rodale, 2009.

Larsen, Earnie. *Stage II Relationships: Love Beyond Addiction.* San Francisco: HarperOne, 1987.

Levine, Stephen. *Unattended Sorrow.* Emmaus, PA: Rodale, 2006.

Lewis, C.S. *The Great Divorce.* San Francisco: HarperOne, 2009.

May, Gerald. *Addiction and Grace: Love and Spirituality in the Healing of Addictions.* San Francisco: HarperOne, 2007.

Millman, Dan. *Way of the Peaceful Warrior,* rev. ed. Tiburon, CA: H.J. Kramer, 2006.

Needleman, Jacob. *Money and the Meaning of Life*. New York: Doubleday, 1994.

Nouwen, Henri, J.M. *Reaching Out: The Three Movements of the Spiritual Life*. New York: Image, 1986.

Pausch, Randy and Jeffrey Zaslow. *The Last Lecture*. New York: Hyperion, 2008.

Peck, M. Scott. *The Road Less Traveled, Twenty-Fifth Anniversary Edition*. New York: Touchstone, 2003.

Ruiz, Miguel. *The Four Agreements: A Practical Guide to Personal Freedom*. Novato, CA: Amber-Allen, 1997.

St. John of the Cross (Mirabai Starr, translator). *Dark Night of the Soul*. New York: Riverhead, 2003.

Siegel, Daniel J. *Mindsight: The New Science of Personal Transformation*. New York: Bantam, 2010.

Small, Jacquelyn. *Awakening in Time: The Journey from Codependence to Co-Creation*. Austin, TX: Eupsychian Press, 1991.

Tillich, Paul. *The Courage to Be*. New Haven, CT: Yale University Press, 2000.

Tolkein, J.R.R. *The Lord of the Rings*. Boston: Houghton Mifflin Harcourt, 2005.

About the Author

Patrick J. Carnes, Ph.D., is an internationally known authority on addiction and recovery issues. He has authored over twenty books including the bestselling titles *Out of the Shadows: Understanding Addiction Recovery, Betrayal Bond, Don't Call It Love*, and *A Gentle Path through the Twelve Steps*, now in an updated and expanded edition. Dr. Carnes's research provides the architecture for the "task model" of treating addictions that is used by thousands of therapists worldwide and many well-known treatment centers, residential facilities, and hospitals. He is the executive director of the Gentle Path Program at Pine Grove Behavioral Health in Hattiesburg, Mississippi, which specializes in dedicated treatment for sexual addiction. For more information on his work and contributions, log on to patrickcarnes.com and sexhelp.com. You can also find him on Facebook and Twitter. For free support and leadership materials, go to www.thetwelveprinciples.com.